PIERRE DEUX'S

BRITTANY

PIERRE DEUX'S
BRITTANY

A French Country Style & Source Book

LINDA DANNENBERG,
PIERRE LEVEC,
AND PIERRE MOULIN

Photographs by Guy Bouchet
Design by Paul Hardy

CLARKSON N. POTTER, INC., PUBLISHERS, NEW YORK

To Benjamin, a great
little traveler who
is always ready for the
next adventure.
—*Linda Dannenberg*

To Denise and Bernard
Cherpitel, who have
opened many doors for
us—including their own,
where we always find
good spirits and good
taste. And to Marcel and
Annie Metzger, for twenty
years of friendship,
generous hospitality, and
professional integrity.
—*"Les Deux Pierre"*

Copyright © 1989 by Linda Dannenberg,
Pierre LeVec, and Pierre Moulin
Photographs copyright © 1989 by Guy
Bouchet

All rights reserved. No part of this book
may be reproduced or transmitted in any
form or by any means, electronic or
mechanical, including photocopying,
recording, or by any information storage and
retrieval system, without permission in
writing from the publisher.

Published by Clarkson N. Potter, Inc.,
and distributed by Crown Publishers, Inc.,
201 East 50th Street,
New York, New York 10022.

CLARKSON N. POTTER, POTTER, and
colophon are trademarks of Clarkson N.
Potter, Inc.

Manufactured in Japan

Library of Congress Cataloging-in-
Publication Data

Dannenberg, Linda.

Pierre Deux's Brittany/Linda
Dannenberg, Pierre LeVec, Pierre
Moulin.

p. cm.

Includes index.

1. Decoration and ornament—France—
Brittany. 2. Brittany (France)—Social life
and customs. I. LeVec, Pierre.
II. Moulin, Pierre.
III. Pierre Deux (Firm) IV. Title.
NK1449.A3B754 1989
745.4′49441—dc19 88-26900
CIP

ISBN 0-517-56436-X
10 9 8 7 6 5 4 3 2 1
First Edition

ACKNOWLEDGMENTS

Brittany made a profound impression on all of us. We were indelibly struck by the intensity of the province—the dramatic landscapes, the awesome seascapes, the dismal-to-dazzling weather that changes with the tides, and the uncompromising rusticity. Most impressive were the people we met along the way: those who cleared the path, introduced us to local specialties, let us into their lives and homes. A life-style book could never exist without them.

For their friendship, cooperation, and advice in Brittany we are most grateful to: Jacques and Colette LeBour; Pierre and Gabrielle Sebilleau; Adolphe and Yvonne Bosser; *les belles étoiles* of La Belle Etoile, Mesdames Paule and Marie-France Raout-Guillou; photographer Pierre Hussenot, who ventured into the enchanted forest of Brocéliande for us; Aline Fouquet; Monsieur Le Bris du Reste and his most helpful team at the Musée Breton in Quimper; Victor Guermeur; Monsieur and Madame Jean de Solminiac; Marie-Renée Offret; Lorraine de Braux; Isabelle and Jean Garçon; Michel and Marie-Josée Pougeard; François and Dominique de Candé; François Vertardier and Caroline Bardin; Judy and Charles-Guy Le Paul; and Jean-Claude Pierpaoli, who received us so graciously at La Mère Poulard.

We would also like to thank members of the Pierre Deux family who willingly took on tasks beyond the call of duty: Serge Bisono, Isabelle Pilate, Fina Bosqued, David Frost, Anka Lefebvre, Barbara Zauft, David Graham, and Robert Diffenderfer.

We are grateful to friends and colleagues in New York for their help in a variety of ways: Lydie Marshall, founder of the celebrated La Bonne Cocotte cooking school, who expertly tested and perfected our recipes; our superb agents, Gayle Benderoff and Deborah Geltman; Spencer Hardy, who furnished us with fine interior photographs needed at the last minute; our helpful liaisons at the French National Tourist Office, Michel Bouquier, George Hern, and Marion Fourestier; Philippe Pascal and Mary Lyons from Food and Wines from France; our imaginative mapmaker Oliver Williams; and Nancy Novogrod, who was present at the conception of the Living in France series and nourished the project early on with her enthusiasm and vision.

A special thanks to Paul Hardy —designer on this book as well as our two previous works, *French Country* and *Pierre Deux's Normandy*—who marries our words and photographs with such imagination and flair.

We would like to express our appreciation to our excellent and most patient editor, Lauren Shakely, who shepherded *Pierre Deux's Brittany* with speed and understanding from early outline to printed tome. For their support, guidance, and inspiration we are also deeply grateful to other friends and colleagues at Clarkson N. Potter and Crown Publishers: Alan Mirken, Bruce Harris, Carol Southern, Gael Towey, Nancy Kahan, Barbara Marks, Michelle Sidrane, Phyllis Fleiss, Jonathan Fox, Anne DeVault, Lisa Lawley, Teresa Nicholas, and Allan Eady.

Finally, our most hearty and heartfelt thanks go to Guy Bouchet, friend and photographer, with whom we've traveled so many miles together. His vision and expertise transform an already beautiful reality into pure magic.

CONTENTS

Ile d' Ouessant

Ile de Batz

Brignogan-Plages

Trégastel-Plage

Ploumanac'h

Ile de Bré

Trébeurden

Perros-Guirec

Po

St-Pol-de-Léon

Tréguier

Pai

Rosanbo

le Folgoët

Morlaix

Guingamp

Plougonven

BREST

CÔTES

le Conquet

Plougastel-Daoulas

Huelgoat

St-Br

Camaret

Brasparts

Cavhaix-Plougu

MONTS D'ARREE

Morgat

Châteaulin

Pleyben

MONTAGNES NOIRES

BAIE DE DOUARNENEZ

Locronan

Ile de Sein

Douarnenez

M

POINTE DU RAZ

CORNOUAILLE

QUIMPER

Pontivy

Audierne

O

R

BAIE D'AUDIERNE

Pont-l'Abbé

Bénodet

Concarneau

Quimperlé

B

St-Guénolé

Beg-Meil

Pont-Aven

Hennebont

le Guilvinec

Port-Manech

le Pouldu

Lorient

Ste-An d'Au

Iles de Glénan

Ile de Groix

Carnac

GOL

Locmar

Quiberon

L'Atlantique

Belle-Ile

Côte d'Emeraude
CAP FREHEL
St-Quay-Portrieux
St-Malo
Cancale
St-Cast-le-Guildo
Dinard
Vallée de la Rance
le Mont-St-Michel
Lamballe
Dinan
NORD
Fougères
ILLE ET VILAINE
RENNES
FORET DE PAIMPONT
Vitré
Châteaubriant
Redon
La Baule
NANTES
Paris

Jutting westward into the Atlantic Ocean, the jagged contours of Brittany's geography reflect the rugged cliffs and outcroppings of its landscape.

MAP BY OLIVER WILLIAMS

PERSPECTIVES

If France were a painter's palette and each province a color, Brittany would be blue. Blue colors Brittany's land- and seascapes, and cleaves to the memory of anyone who visits here even for a short time.

The blues of Brittany are sometimes so vivid that they force all other colors into a mottled backdrop. There must be a hundred shades of this pervasive color, from the classic French blue trim on the trawlers docked at Lesconil to the deep blue water at high tide in Belon; from the aquamarine of the hand-tied fishnets—the famous *filets bleus*—of Concarneau to the electric blue of the octagonal lobster traps in Morlaix; from the navy blue sails of a schooner off of Roscoff to the whimsically painted sky blue *deux-chevaux* Citroën parked in Pont-Aven. Every hue and tint is represented, each intense against the somber Breton setting where the various grays of granite, slate, and a stormy sky predominate. Nature's achromatic scale puts the Brittany blues into high relief.

Brittany is a land of contrasts. Just as one becomes resigned to days of cool, leaden weather, the tide will turn (literally), bringing two days of such dazzling clarity that they seem like a vision of heaven. The good days are especially spectacular because there are generally so few of them. The topography can change as suddenly as the weather, with a bend in the road. Two minutes from the flat, scrubby, seaside outskirts of La Forêt-Fouesnant brings one deep into the town's enchanted forest. Driving inland, away from the forest, one is soon in the midst of rolling heaths blooming with heather. The Armor and the Argoat ("the country near the sea" and "the country of wood") are the names the Gauls gave to the two faces of Brittany. There is also the formal geographic division of the province into Upper Brittany and Lower Brittany. The line of demarcation runs north to south, separating Brittany into eastern and western segments. Upper Brittany is the eastern, more sophisticated half, closer to Paris, where French has always been spoken. Lower Brittany, the wilder and more isolated western part, is the prow-shaped area that juts into the sea, where, until the early 20th century, Breton was spoken almost exclusively.

Contrasts in Brittany permeate even the language. Up and down the Atlantic coast and for many miles inland, the elegance and precision of French is juxtaposed with the tongue-twisting glottal syllables of Breton, a language closely related to Welsh that testifies to Brittany's deep Celtic roots. Throughout Brittany (*Breiz* in Breton) towns have such names as Plougastel-Daoulas, Lampaul-Ploudalmézeau, and Aber-Wrac'h, populated by people named Gwenaëlle, Guénolé, and Löic.

Each region of Brittany is distinctive, with its own landscape, style, traditions, and even weather. The north coast along the English Channel, divided into the

After mass on Sunday morning, the old women of Pont-l'Abbé, left, many of whom continue to wear the region's tall white *coiffe*, exchange the latest news before returning home. Charming half-timbered houses line the streets of old Quimper, above left. A visitor's bicycle rests outside the Musée du Pont-Aven during a special centenary exhibition of Gauguin's local works.

Pink Granite Coast and the Emerald Coast, is craggy and dramatic, with weather that is gray and cool more often than not. Several old dowager resorts, such as Dinard, were developed here in the late 19th century for a wealthy English clientele. This is the only part of Brittany to achieve the kind of fashionable allure enjoyed by Normandy, its neighbor to the north. Farther south, in the Morbihan *département*, warm sunlight and temperate breezes wash over the Iles du Morbihan, the seaside health spa in Quiberon, and the sprawling, modern resort of La Baule, with its high-rise *résidences* and the longest white sand beach in France. Just inland from the Quiberon peninsula, in the town of Carnac, lie fields of megalithic monuments as haunting as those of England's Stonehenge. Deep in Brittany's interior, fields, pastures, and a modest mountain or two stretch out in all directions from Rennes, a university town and the capital of Brittany. Cornouaille, the province's midcoastal region, is the most traditional, a land that still retains the old customs, costumes, and folklore festivals. For the visitor, this is the quintessential Brittany of *coiffes*, crêpes, and old-fashioned fishing villages.

A roiling, restless ocean, here photographed off Belle-Ile in the Morbihan, is both friend and foe to the Bretons who take their livelihood from the sea. "A very old male monster" is how Pierre Jakez Hélias, the eminent chronicler of traditional Breton life, above, describes the Breton's view of the sea. Overleaf: The Aulne River winds through the little inland town of Châteaulin, dreamlike on an early spring morning.

T he blues of Brittany, such as these photographed in the Finistère *département*, enhance the province's somber natural palette with a dazzling array of shades and tints. The most common color for fishing boats is a bright French blue, with leftover paint used to freshen up doors and shutters of the fishermen's cottages—one reason why this shade seems ubiquitous. Even the Citroën has taken on the appropriate Breton hue.

Boats—large and small, for work and for pleasure—crowd Brittany's many small picturesque harbors.

The thickly wooded property of a 17th-century château near the Mont Saint-Michel, left, shields the house from almost every perspective. From the Mont Saint-Michel, right, to south Finistère, the richly varied terrain of Brittany forms a colorful mosaic.

The haunting stones of Carnac, the Morbihan island town with more than three thousand megaliths, date from 50,000 to 2000 B.C. They appear in all sorts of configurations, from long ranks of tall stones, called *menhirs*, above and below right, to *dolmens*, right, table-like arrangements of boulders thought to be burial chambers.

HISTORIC BRITTANY

Although histories of Brittany often begin with the arrival of the Gauls in about 500 B.C., there is evidence of an important prehistoric civilization that existed thousands of years before the Gauls set foot in the province. In Carnac alone there are more than 3,000 megaliths, carefully arranged in a variety of configurations. The oldest megalithic stone has been carbon-dated to 4600 B.C. Many interpretations have been offered for the monumental legacies. Whether they were solar calendars, astronomic systems for predicting eclipses, or perhaps pathways to huge temples of a sun cult, we will probably never know. But one fact is indisputable: the megaliths are as solidly in place today as they were when they greeted the Gauls in the first millennium.

In 57 B.C. Julius Caesar and his armies vanquished the powerful Veneti tribe, descendants of the Gauls, and thus conquered the country. Armor was a calm outpost of Roman civilization until the first barbarian invasions in 277 A.D. By the 5th century, everything the Romans had created had been destroyed.

The roots of today's Brittany took hold in the year 460, with the immigration of refugee Celts who were driven from their homes in Britain by the Angles and the Saxons. Armor was rechristened "Little Britain," and shortly thereafter came to be known as Brittany. In the following centuries Brittany became a duchy under Charlemagne, then an independent dynasty that survived a massive Norman invasion in the 10th century. Brittany finally became a part of France when Claude of France, daughter

of Duchesse Anne of Brittany, married the future king, François I, in 1514. She subsequently ceded the duchy of Brittany to the dauphin, and the final union with France was proclaimed in 1532.

Until modern times linked Brittany irrevocably to Paris, the province had contact with the outside world via the sea—the source of livelihood on the one hand, and the remorseless taker of life on the other. Brittany was known as a poor and isolated

province of great superstition and little culture. While the larger cities, such as Rennes, Quimper, and Morlaix, had aristocratic and wealthy bourgeois inhabitants, the coast and interior farmlands were populated by peasants and fishermen who led humble, hard lives of punishing work and little leisure. In a land of granite, winds, and fierce tides, nothing comes easy. The church, which the Bretons embraced with almost mystical fervor, was the only escape from the drudgery of daily life.

The great clipper ships, returning to port after months or years in foreign waters, carried with them news and cargo from far-off lands. The inhabitants of Lower Brittany were often more *au courant* about events in the East Indies than the latest happenings in Paris. Only with World Wars I and II did Brittany's long isolation end. Breton soldiers discovered the rest of Europe, while Allied and occupying forces brought to Brittany glimpses of the world beyond its boundaries.

Eleven standing stones support a monumental slab in the *dolmen*, right, at Crucuno, a small village north of Carnac.

There is an old Breton saying that goes, "Bretons are born with the waters of the sea flowing 'round their hearts." The farming communities of the interior notwithstanding, Brittany is first and foremost a maritime province. "Deep in the heart of the countryside," notes Pierre Jakez Hélias, Brittany's leading contemporary writer and the oracle on Breton life, "the wind still smells of the sea."

While women traditionally worked the land, men worked the sea, setting out on voyages that sometimes lasted as long as seven years. Breton respect for the ocean is profound, their marine skills incomparable.

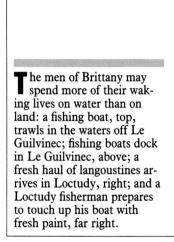

The men of Brittany may spend more of their waking lives on water than on land: a fishing boat, top, trawls in the waters off Le Guilvinec; fishing boats dock in Le Guilvinec, above; a fresh haul of langoustines arrives in Loctudy, right; and a Loctudy fisherman prepares to touch up his boat with fresh paint, far right.

Local fishing boats, above, right, and below, come in all shapes, sizes, and colors—from modest dinghies to large trawlers.

At five in the afternoon, a fisherman in Loctudy, top, unloads his catch. Off the coast of Le Guilvinec, fishermen still haul in their nets by hand, above. Coiled nets, left, wait on deck for a day's outing at sea.

 Breton sea-rescue teams are renowned throughout Europe, and the sailors and fishermen of Brittany are proud of their reputation. They like to say that in French, the sea, *la mer*, is feminine, while in Breton the sea, *mor*, is masculine.

Voyages are shorter these days, lasting hours or weeks rather than years. Boats of all sizes ply the waters, from small wooden *barques* with outboard motors to mammoth oceangoing vessels. Forty-one percent of France's fish is brought into Breton ports. Aside from the port of Saint-Malo in the north, where the cod-fishing industry is centralized, most of the important harbors —Concarneau, Lorient, Douarnenez, Le Guilvinec, Saint-Guénolé, Loctudy, La Turballe, Le Croisic, and Camaret-sur-Mer —are on the south coast.

Daily fishing boats, which work the inshore waters, sailing out and returning with the tide, bring in langoustines (small saltwater crawfish), scallops, sole, turbot, sardines, mackerel, and sea bass. The big trawlers that fish for weeks at a time, in waters as far away as Ireland, return with their holds filled with tuna, cod, and lobsters. At each port a *criée*, or fish auction, begins as soon as the boats unload.

Graffiti from the 18th-century, above, still mark a lichen-covered boulder in a Morbihan cove. An empty wooden boat moored in a motionless saltwater pond has the otherworldly beauty of pure form, right. Overleaf: The colorful quay is near Audierne.

MERLIN, MYTHS, AND MAGIC

Inspired by her Druid legacy, her Celtic heritage, her long years of isolation, or perhaps a combination of all three factors, Brittany is a land rife with legend, superstition, and myth. Good and evil spirits, gnomes, fairies, and phantoms populate the lore of the Breton countryside, as do noble ladies, princes, magicians, and kings. Brocéliande, the deep and primeval forest setting for many adventures of King Arthur and his knights of the Round Table, was the former name of today's Paimpont Forest, on the north coast of Brittany. Here Merlin the sorcerer fell in love with the fairy Viviane, who trapped him in an enchanted circle to be hers forever. And here Sir Galahad, the son of Lancelot, finally found the Holy Grail.

In southern Brittany on the Penmarc'h peninsula, Tristan and Iseult played out their tragic love story. King Mark of Cornouaille dispatched Tristan to Ireland to bring back Iseult, the king's intended bride. On board the ship returning from Ireland, Tristan and Iseult mistakenly drank a love potion intended for the newlyweds after the royal wedding. The hapless young couple, bound in eternal love, were doomed to separate. Tristan eventually married another Iseult, but never stopped longing for his true love. Years later, gravely wounded in battle, Tristan sent couriers to find Iseult. If the mission succeeded, the ship bearing her to him was to return under white sails; if it failed, black sails. As the ship approached through heavy fog, Tristan's jealous wife assured him that the sails, which were white, were actually black. Disappointment and a broken heart hastened Tristan's death. Iseult, arriving too late, lay down to die beside him.

Among the multitude of elves and gnomes that populate Brittany are *korrigans*, *farfadets*, *korils*, and *poulpiquets*. These creatures are mostly benign, although sometimes capricious and occasionally jealous like Viviane. It was believed that they could occasionally be glimpsed joking and dancing by the light of the moon. But dealing with these little beings involves certain caveats and traditions. One should never dance with a *korrigan* because he can make you lose track of time; you'll wake up in twenty years with a white beard. And it is always a good idea to leave a crêpe or a glass of milk on the table at night for the fairies who might drop down the chimney to help with the housework or the spinning. Brittany's phantoms mainly haunt the most desolate areas. On the Ile de Sein, a tiny island off the coast of Audierne, it is said that a great phantom ship appearing through the fog at dawn is an omen of an imminent shipwreck.

In the tiny village church of Tréhorenteuc, deep in the forest of Paimpont, a tall stained-glass window created in 1943 illustrates the legendary moment in the 6th century when a vision of the Holy Grail—a chalice holding drops of Christ's blood—appeared to King Arthur and his knights gathered at the Round Table. The apparition of the grail was the inspiration for Arthur's life-long quest for this elusive object, thought to have been lost in Brittany in the forest of Brocéliande a few years after the death of Christ. (Photo: Pierre Hussenot)

From the site of the Rocher des Faux Amants (Rock of False Lovers)—some 558 feet tall—the witch Morgana cast spells on young men who betrayed their ladies. (Photo: Pierre Hussenot)

eligion deeply permeates traditional Breton life. In Brittany's rural past it provided diversion on Sundays, and especially on feast and festival days; counsel or recourse in the face of problems; and solace in times of (usually seaborne) disaster. In addition to the traditional Catholic saints, rural Bretons had a large roster of "healing saints," most of whom were never canonized by the church. Provincial icons rather than austere religious symbols, these "saints" could be approached like old friends. Among them were Saint Livertin, who cured headaches, and Saint Tugen, whose key helped drive away mad dogs.

The profound religiosity of the Bretons is symbolized most powerfully by the impressive, carved-granite Calvaires that loom above the landscape of Brittany from coast to hinterland. The Calvaires, usually set within a parish close, are massive representations of Christ on the Cross, surrounded by scores of sculpted figures and scenes from the Passion and life of Christ. Most were constructed between the 14th and 17th centuries and were used by the parish priests to instruct illiterate villagers.

Another example of Brittany's compelling religious faith is the local *pardon*, a traditional pageant held annually in many Breton communities. The crowds of believers and tourists attending these events can be huge, drawn by the torchlight processions, the open-air masses and benedictions by the sea.

In the churchyard of Plozévet, a small village west of Quimper, a memorial plaque, top, commemorates the loss of a shipload of valiant men in a battle against the English in the Napoleonic Wars. Among the most imposing Calvaires are those depicting the entire Crucifixion scene, above. Marking an obscure rural crossroads deep in the Monts d'Arée region of central Brittany is a 14th-century Calvaire, left. Less stylized than the Calvaire on this page, it is deeply affecting in its grave simplicity.

A detail of a 15th-century Calvaire in a village in Cornouaille, left, depicts the Passion of Christ. Members of a parish in north Finistère, below, prepare for a *pardon*, an annual religious festival.

The colorful and elaborate
embroidery unique to
Pont-l'Abbé adorns a traditional, turn-of-the-century
jacket, top, saved for Sundays
and holidays. A detail of a
late 19th-century *lit clos*, or
box bed, above, in a house in
the outskirts of Pont-l'Abbé,
is decorated with the carved
geometric designs and brass
studs popular in the region.
As with many similar pieces
of furniture, one spindle is set
in upside-down in the belief
that nothing but God should
be perfect. Another *lit clos*,
from Morlaix on the north
coast, shows how the curtains
could be drawn for winter-
time warmth, right.

THE STYLE OF BRITTANY

Brittany's isolation inspired a fascinating local style, since, unlike most other provinces of France, it was almost free of outside influences. So removed was most of Brittany from Parisian trends that the province might as well have been in another country, or on another planet. Rustic, even rude, Breton style was founded on practicality and durability. There was little concern for or even knowledge of "good taste." Form was imposed by function, climate, and necessity.

Most of the classic furniture of Brittany is heavy, massive, somber, and geometric. The most characteristic pieces are the *lits clos* (the box beds sometimes large enough for a family of four), voluminous linen

The serpentine form of the chest, above, and its fancy brass pulls and locks, mark it as a piece influenced by Parisian cabinetmakers. A remarkably graphic 17th-century grotesque above a doorway in Locronan, right, captures the eye.

An old rocking horse rests atop a typical carved Breton armoire once used to store a family's finery, far left. Stone construction, sometimes punctuated by gabled dormers, left, is the hallmark of Breton architecture.

The elegant scalloped back-rest of a three-seat settee is echoed by an equally sophisticated apron, but the woven rush seat and the backdrop of stonework and hydrangeas give away the piece's country origin.

chests, sideboards, armoires, clock cases, and étagères. Crafted by artisans working at home in their barns, the furniture was usually created from oak, particularly in Lower Brittany, as well as from chestnut, walnut, cherry, or even wood salvaged from shipwrecks. Rectangular and boxlike in form, the pieces were often lavishly carved over their facades, as if to compensate for the simplicity of shape. Hearts, birds, geometric designs, and religious symbols adorn pieces from the 17th and 18th centuries, as do Celtic motifs, grapes, and daisies. Furniture from the 19th century was decorated with carved spindles and shining yellow-copper studs. Furniture created in Upper Brittany, in or near

In the traditional modest Breton home, antique spoon racks such as the one holding a family's decorated copper spoons, left, were usually suspended above the dining table. A large model boat in the Musée Bigouden in Pont-l'Abbé, above, was carried in the Blessing of the Sea procession. An 18th-century Breton *égouttoir* (drying rack) today serves as a decorative étagère, right. (Photos: Spencer Hardy)

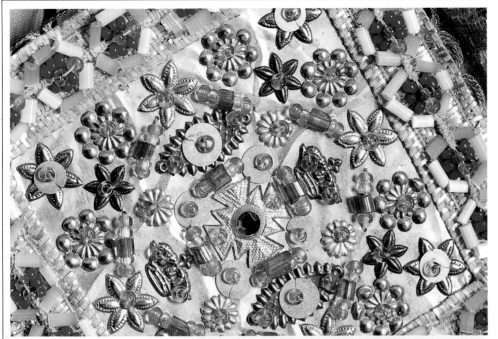

Intricate beadwork embellishes a 19th-century vest from Cornouaille, above, now in the collection of the Musée Breton in Quimper. The jacket of a 19th-century cavalry officer rests on the back of a chair, right, in the Château de Rosanbo near Brittany's north coast, as if the young military man had just returned from the war.

Rennes, was more supple, sculptural, and harmonious—in a word, elegant—than the products of the rest of the province. Lighter woods, such as pear and beech, were used for armoires with curving cornices, fluid lines, and gracefully rounded feet. In both parts of the province, but particularly in Lower Brittany, cupboards came with *niches de dévotion*—tiny alcoves where a ceramic Saint Anne, the patron saint of Brittany, or a statue of the Virgin, could be displayed.

Most of the furniture in a typical, modest Breton dwelling could usually be found in one room—the common room where the family ate and slept, where armoires, *lits clos*, and chests stood end to end against one wall. Because of this unusual arrangement, unique to Brittany, the backs and sides of the furniture were frequently left plain, or even unfinished, since they would never be seen—a useful fact for the antique hunter.

Like the purest of Breton furniture, the Breton house is a model of simplicity and solidity. The plan is rectangular, the material granite and slate, the decorative detailing almost nonexistent. Until the 15th century, the half-timbered house topped by

Hand-carved wooden shoes, right, were the footwear of choice throughout rural Brittany up until the end of World War II. They are still worn occasionally by participants in folkloric festivals. A romantic blue-and-white painted *lit clos* from the island of Ouessant promises a cozy night's sleep, far right.

a straw-thatched roof was almost as popular in Brittany as it was in Normandy. Then the style began to fade in favor of fire-resistant stone. There are still vestiges of half-timbered construction in the old towns of Dinan, Morlaix, and Quimper.

The traditional rural home in Brittany was generally sited with the front facade facing south. The north wall was blind—windowless—to minimize the north wind's chill. The two sides were usually blind as well, since the chimneys were located there. The front of the house had one centered wooden door, sometimes brightly painted, and several small windows, all bordered with hand-hewn granite blocks. Until the 19th century few windows were glazed, and shutters were not just a finishing touch but an essential practical feature for keeping out wind and rain. Since the floors were often of *terre battue* (beaten earth), the houses had no cellars, but most did have attics tucked under their slate or thatched roofs.

To construct stone walls, masons used smaller and smaller stones on the upper courses—a very practical technique that avoided the necessity of hoisting the heaviest stones ten to thirty feet. In keeping with rural custom, the first stone of a house was usually set in place and marked with a cross on a Saturday night so that the dawning of Sunday would bless it.

A closeup of an elaborately carved and inlaid armoire by a local craftsman, left, shows the inscription, "Made by me, Louis Pati, 1820." The spindle work of the *vaisselier* (dishrack), right, protects a collection of faience.

BRITTANY'S COUNTRY COOKING

The hardworking Bretons ate to live, and their recipes reflect this pragmatic culinary approach. Dishes such as the *cotriade*, a savory Breton fish stew; buckwheat crêpes filled with cheese, onions, or ham; or the *kouign-amann*, a dense rich cake made from flour, butter, powdered sugar, and an egg yolk, are more straightforward than elegant. Yet because their flavor comes from basic ingredients simply prepared, they are deeply satisfying.

In this province, where fishermen haul in almost half the fish and shellfish of France, menus of local restaurants not surprisingly favor seafood, but there are other fine regional specialties to choose from as well. Frequently listed is the delicious and distinctive *pré-salé* lamb, whose meat owes its flavor to the salt grasses of the coastal marshlands where the sheep graze. There are also ducks from the region of Nantes and meaty chicken from Rennes, prepared in a variety of fruit, wine, and herb sauces.

Brittany has no wines of its own, but the region has adopted Muscadet, from the Melon de Bourgogne grape, and Gros Plant, from the Folle Blanche grape, appellations produced just beyond the border of Brittany near Nantes, in the Loire Valley. These pale gold, dry white wines comple-

Few foods are more symbolic of the versatility and simple elegance of Breton cooking than the traditional four-cornered buckwheat crêpe. At its most basic, served with jam and sparkling cider, it is a satisfying light lunch.

ment perfectly Brittany's seafood platters. Locally produced sparkling cider, lightly alcoholic and very refreshing, is the other favored beverage in Brittany, particularly in the central and northern parts of the region. Cider accompanies traditional lamb and poultry dishes surprisingly well, while it is the perfect foil, dry and just slightly effervescent, for sweet or savory crêpes.

Long maligned by gourmets for its lack of gastronomic flair, Brittany has recently received overdue attention in the realm of fine food. There are now chefs in Brittany from La Baule to Cancale whose imaginative and skillful use of the region's fine basic ingredients soars far beyond the traditional. Michelin stars have risen over more than a dozen of these establishments, including the Moulin de Rosmadec in Pont-Aven, the Hotel du Goyen in Audierne, and in double magnitude over Château de Locguénolé in Hennebont. With a major increase in tourism since the war, there is now a sophisticated, affluent, and hungry clientele ready to pay for and appreciate sublime regional fare, and Breton chefs have risen to the challenge. While not alto-

gether abandoning the standard repertoire of raw seafood platters, baked fish, and stewed lamb, Brittany's elite chefs are gilding their menus with such fare as *sabayon citronné de moruette* (scrod in lemon sabayon), *huîtres farcies aux amandes* (stuffed oysters with almonds), and *galettes de sarrassin au crabe, beurre curry* (buckwheat crêpes stuffed with crab in curry butter served in a sea-urchin shell). The late French gastronome and critic Curnonsky (pen name of Maurice Edmond Sailland), who adopted Brittany as his second home and visited frequently throughout the twenties, thirties, and forties, always enthusiastically boosted Breton cooking. "For fifty years," Curnonsky wrote late in his life, "I have been shouting from the rooftops that the gastronomy of Brittany is admirable, though misunderstood, if not altogether unknown." He especially would rejoice in the changes that have transpired over the last three decades in Breton cooking.

A rustic farm table in a kitchen on the Mont Saint-Michel, above, displays fresh local vegetables and fruits. Cartons of raspberries from nearby farms, right, are a motif in produce markets.

Brittany's succulent *belon* and *fine de claire* oysters, left, are rivals in the realm of exquisite taste. These pearly morsels are best consumed in the harbor on the day of the harvest, although they are sometimes air-shipped to oyster bars and seafood restaurants in the United States.

Concentric circles of thinly sliced apples, left, top the delectable tart prepared by Chef Pierre Sebilleau of the Moulin de Rosmadec in Pont-Aven (see pages 152–157). *Gâteaux bretons*, above, are Brittany's traditional rich and crumbly butter cookies.

LE MONT SAINT-MICHEL

Walking late at night along the ramparts of Mont Saint-Michel evokes the enduring power of this daunting monument, acclaimed as one of the wonders of the world.

Le Mont Saint-Michel is to France," Victor Hugo said, "what the Great Pyramid is to Egypt." By dusk, the crowds that swarm up and down the Mont have departed, and the wind can be heard whispering across the medieval stones. Humbled by the indomitable silhouette of the abbey rising toward the firmament, one can only give silent homage to the human ingenuity and effort it took to create this wondrous place.

Located precisely on the border between Normandy and Brittany, Mont Saint-Michel has been claimed and disputed by both provinces for centuries. To cloud the issue even further, the Mont is in both the Michelin guide to Normandy and the Michelin guide to Brittany, although for voting purposes it is officially designated as Normandy. The Breton writer Pierre Jakez Hélias, ever a diplomat, told us that at high tide,

separated from the land, it is in Normandy, while at low tide, with access to the coast, it is in Brittany.

Pilgrims have been converging on Mont Saint-Michel for hundreds of years, in spite of the dangerous, swirling, irregular tides that sweep in at 210 feet a minute, covering the sands and occasionally trapping the unwary still making their way across the six-mile expanse from the mainland. Today a long causeway straight to the Mont's enormous parking lot at the base eliminates any problem of access, except at the highest tides, for the almost 1 million visitors each year.

Between darkness and dawn the island is left to its residents and a handful of fortunate overnight visitors. Sunsets here are particularly spectacular, but the best moments are those under moonlight. It is in these quiet, shadowed hours of night that the Mont—isolated, silent, majestic—truly prevails.

At low tide, left, the Mont Saint-Michel is beached in a sea of sand. For most of its history, until the 20th-century addition of a causeway, the island was accessible only when the tide, which can recede as far as ten miles, was out. The region's famous *pré-salé* or salt-marsh lambs, above, noted for their unique flavor, graze within view of the Mont.

THE TOWN

With terrain so severely limited on the Mont, houses and shops grew up and out wherever a square meter became available, even if it happened to be twenty or thirty feet in the air. The buildings that line the narrow, cobblestoned Grande Rue—the Mont's only street—most dating from the 15th and 16th centuries, are a fascinating pastiche of shingles, stonework, variegated rooflines, turrets, gables, exposed beams, and cantilevered extensions. Most of the shops specialize in inexpensive souvenirs, just as they did in the 1400s when pilgrims treasured religious mementos of their trek. Even today, few visitors are able to leave Mont Saint-Michel empty-handed.

The Gothic spires of the Saint-Michel abbey loom above the homes of the densely built granite structures of the town at dusk, left. The handsome stone houses of this community sheltered within the medieval ramparts bear witness to the skilled craftsmanship of 15th- and 16th-century masons, above and right.

The Mont Saint-Michel is an architectural wonder from a distance; close up, it is a tapestry of shapes and textures. Granite, slate, wood shingles, and brick in the form of squares, rectangles, scallops, and cones make this old town that grew up between the 15th and 18th centuries a memorable visual treat for the visitor.

MONT-SAINT-MICHEL
TELEGRAPHE
POSTE.TELEPHONE

The structure of the Mont Saint-Michel, right, consists of so many layers that it is almost impossible to imagine how it was built.

THE ABBEY

The history of the abbey of Mont Saint-Michel reaches back to the year 708, when the archangel Michael appeared to Aubert, bishop of Avranches in Normandy, and commanded that a sanctuary dedicated to Saint Michael be constructed on the nearby Mont Tombe, the site of Druidic worship, which shortly thereafter was renamed Mont Saint-Michel. Rock by rock, year by year, the early Benedictine oratory took form. To achieve the construction, granite blocks had to be ferried in from the Chausey Islands off Normandy or carried by cart from the north coast of Brittany, and then hauled up 258 feet to the island's peak. The original oratory was first replaced by a Carolingian abbey, and then, in the 11th century, by the Romanesque monastery that stands today. During the 13th century, five halls and a cloister were created in the Gothic style on the north side of the Mont, an ensemble of such beauty and architectural splendor that it came to be known as La Merveille (the Marvel). In the 15th century, monks added a superb Gothic choir.

After 1789, the abbey became a prison, the revolutionaries renaming the island Mont Libre (Free Mount). In 1863 Napoleon III abolished the prison and in 1874 the abbey and ramparts became *monuments historiques* and were restored by the state.

The Gothic spires of the Saint-Michel abbey, built between the 13th and 16th centuries, face the east and the rising sun. From the top of the abbey the figure of Saint Michael surveys the sea and surrounding countryside, inset left.

The awesome interior of the abbey church encompasses a Romanesque nave and transept dating to the late 11th century, and a Gothic chancel built by Benedictine monks between 1450 and 1521. The wizardry of the medieval architects is best appreciated in this view of the web of buttresses and arches that support the clerestory and the massive ceiling.

The choir, in the Flamboyant style, is surrounded by small chapels and Gothic-arched aisles. Elaborate flying buttresses support the domed ceiling and separate the intricately designed windows that flood the church with shimmering celestial light.

The abbey's cloister, above and right, part of the enclave of Gothic structures called La Merveille—"The Marvel"—is among the most famed and popular of the abbey's attractions. More than 200 elegantly carved columns of red granite support the sculpted arcade of white limestone decorated with botanical motifs that surrounds the courtyard. Here monks once meditated and prayed among the sweet-smelling herbs and sharp-scented boxwood that filled the courtyard garden.

LA MÈRE POULARD

Omelette" hardly suffices to describe the huge, billowing creations that have made La Mère Poulard famous for more than one hundred years. The hotel-restaurant has occupied the same spot at the base of Mont Saint-Michel's main street since it was founded. Here, in the rustic atmosphere of massive beams, hewn stone walls, and red-checked tablecloths, countless omelettes have risen like soufflés from copper skillets held over crackling wood fires. As versatile as the Breton crêpe, the omelette may be ordered as an appetizer, as the main course, or sugared and flambéed, as a triumphant dessert.

At La Mère Poulard, the flush-faced cooks beat out a syncopated rhythm with their large whisks as primitive as that of jungle drums: da-da–DUM da-da–DUM da-da-da-da-da-da–DUM. The sound can be heard well down the road and is as memorable a part of a visit to La Mère Poulard as the omelettes themselves.

Their whisking arms briefly at rest, two omelette beaters in the kitchen of La Mère Poulard await the next orders for the restaurant's celebrated dish, as much a feature of Mont Saint-Michel as the abbey itself.

L'OMELETTE DE LA MERE POULARD

- **2 large eggs**
- **½ teaspoon salt**
  Pepper
- **3 ounces (¾ stick) salted butter**

Break the eggs into a large unlined copper bowl. Using a balloon whisk, beat the eggs until frothy, then add the salt and lots of freshly ground pepper.

Continue beating the eggs until they have quadrupled in volume and hold their shape but are not stiff.

Melt the butter over low heat in a 9-inch tin-lined copper skillet or copper sauté pan and add the eggs. Watch the omelette carefully and occasionally run a fork around the edges. Briefly remove the pan from the heat from time to time to keep the bottom of the omelette from drying out.

The omelette should rise like a soufflé.

When the omelette is set but still moist, slide it onto a preheated platter. Fold the omelette over and serve immediately.

NOTE: *The basic omelette can be dressed up by sprinkling a variety of fillings over the omelette as it cooks.*

Serves 1

The steps in omelette making are few, but they require practiced skills: at left, an expert beater whips three eggs at a time with a balloon whisk. In the copper pan the omelette then puffs and browns over a wood fire, inset far right. Delicately crusted on the outside, moist and airy as a soufflé on the inside, an omelette à La Mère Poulard, far right, is a treat for all the senses. Jean-Claude Pierpaoli, maître d' of La Mère Poulard and, for the more than thirty years he has been working at the restaurant, an acquaintance of Pierre Moulin, prepares to serve a dessert omelette garnished with fruit preserve, right.

64

The monolithic appearance of the house protects its owners' privacy. Oblivious to the home's attractions or even its existence, a constant flow of tourists eager to visit the abbey and the ramparts passes by the mullioned windows of this unusual residence all day long. A few schoolchildren even have the energy to scale the Mont at a run.

Napoleon III, who transformed the Mont Saint-Michel abbey into a protected landmark rather than a functioning religious institution, the house came into the possession of two families of fishermen, who over the years were less than exacting in its maintenance.

By the time a military nurse named Mademoiselle Marie Provost, aunt of the present owner, bought the house, the interiors were grimy and worn. She cleared, scrubbed, restored, and furnished the rooms, making the house an inviting, comfortable, family-style abode where she welcomed many relatives and friends. One of her frequent visitors for many years was Maréchal Pétain, a friend from World War I, who stayed for a week or two every summer. Mademoiselle Provost never married, although it was apparently not for lack of offers: she refused, the owners say, seventy-two marriage proposals in her lifetime. When she died in 1943, she bequeathed the house to her niece and the niece's husband, who live there today.

Mademoiselle Provost, left, posed for this picture in her World War I nurse's uniform. An intriguing collection of Mont Saint-Michel photographs, books, and memorabilia, right, fills a stone alcove set into a living room wall. The owners have an even larger collection in their Paris pied-à-terre so that, wherever they reside, the Mont Saint-Michel is at hand.

Their five children have spent virtually all of their vacations on the Mont, and the tradition continues now with grandchildren. The tradition of notable houseguests continues as well; Birendra, the king of Nepal, a family friend made during government service in the Far East, has visited on several occasions.

Although they divide their time between Paris and Mont Saint-Michel, the owners are voting citizens of the Mont, which long ago captured their hearts. The couple recently celebrated their fiftieth wedding anniversary with a service in the abbey among family and friends. They have amassed an enormous collection of Mont Saint-Michel memorabilia, ranging from faded 19th-century postcards and souvenir medallions to antique guidebooks. While a part of the collection remains on the Mont, most of the pieces fill bookshelves and cover the walls of their home in Paris. Thus, even when they are four hours away from Mont Saint-Michel, they are still surrounded by its images and artifacts.

The large kitchen is in the oldest wing of the house, which dates from the 14th century, but the built-in dark oak cupboards were added in the mid-19th century. The simple furnishings include a large rustic farm table, assorted stools and chairs, and a tall *tiroir à épices* (spice cabinet) set by a doorway.

A shining collection of antique copperware—many pieces from Villedieu-les-Poêles in Normandy, others from England—hangs against the wood-and-stone kitchen walls, left and right. The two largest pieces, mounted on wood above the table at left, are a basin and water reservoir, which save trips to the well for washing hands. A *tripière*, a vessel for serving tripe, sits on the table.

The 19th-century living room, designed in 1828, was restored and furnished by Marie Provost, the aunt of the current lady of the house, just after World War I.

An unusual 19th-century daybed in the living room, inset with two bookshelves, is upholstered with 19th-century toile de Jouy fabric featuring a pastoral landscape with classical monuments.

A late 19th-century oriental-print cotton toile covers an alcove bed flanked by two closets in one of several upstairs bedrooms, left. The cut-and-crocheted linen curtains were stitched by Marie Provost. In a first-floor bedroom behind the kitchen, above, a family armoire dating from 1839 holds old linens.

densely wooded glen. Constructed of granite or shale, many *petits manoirs* and farmhouses sit exposed in the center of an open meadow. For the same climatic reasons, windows are larger than in other parts of Brittany, and there are more of them. The most imposing dwellings often boast a second floor and an attic covered by a roof set with dormer windows, a style that came into vogue in the rural houses of this area in the 18th century.

To the west of Saint-Brieuc, in north Finistère, is the intriguing town of Morlaix. A thriving port town in 1505 when Queen Anne of Brittany paid homage there to the saints, it continues to thrive today as a market town rather than a shipping center. The once extremely active port is now used mainly for pleasure boats.

An omnipresent feature of the Breton shore are lichen-covered boulders, above. A sailing club on the coast near Roscoff, right, stores its gear in a small, worn cottage with two tiny chimneys, harmonious in its simplicity.

Seen from atop a railway bridge in Morlaix are the diverse slate roofs of this market town's old center, a cluster of buildings that spans four centuries. The numerous chimney pots testify to Brittany's winter chill, chased away by many a roaring fire.

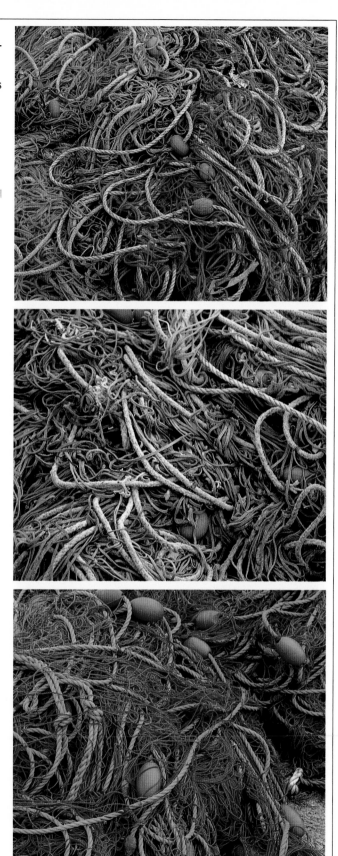

Marée basse (low tide), left, completely clears the Roscoff harbor of water. Local fishermen go home to eat and sleep while recreational sailors use the enforced time in port to dry their clothes and sails and improve their tans. The nets of Roscoff fishermen, right, are a poetic tangle of ropes and lines, seaweed and buoys after the day's fishing.

SAINT-MALO

At one point during the Middle Ages, Saint-Malo, then controlled by a bishopric, declared itself a republic and adopted the watchword *"Ni français, ni breton, malouin suis"* (neither a Frenchman nor a Breton am I, but a man of Saint-Malo). An ancient, walled city surrounded by 13th-century ramparts, Saint-Malo, named after a 6th-century Welsh saint, was badly damaged by a bombing raid in August 1944. Most of the old city of Saint-Malo was devastated. After the war, the citizens regrouped, gathered their resources, and restored the old city, virtually down to the last stone. The old city is almost entirely surrounded by water, and in fact, the site of Saint-Malo was originally an island; today a spit and a broad roadway connect it to the mainland.

Buffeted by strong North Atlantic winds, sailboats —spinnakers hoisted—race in the Saint-Malo harbor in view of the ramparts and the meticulously restored city, begun in the 12th century. Even as a pastime, sailing in Brittany is a rugged activity, requiring skill, stamina, and protective gear, above. (Photos: Pierre Hussenot)

DINAN

Just inland on the Rance River from Saint-Malo lies Dinan, one of the oldest fortified towns in Brittany. Surrounded by ramparts, the city has a distinctly medieval look, with cobbled streets of 15th- and 16th-century half-timbered houses and shops, a 14th-century château rising above the town, and a 14th-century gate leading into its oldest sector. Even in the 14th century Dinan had a romantic aspect: it was here that Du Guesclin met his future wife, Tiphaine Raguenel. While its more fashionable neighbor, Dinard, draws beach lovers and a society crowd, Dinan draws history and architecture buffs, and lovers of all things quaint.

Scenes of Dinan, a river town near Brittany's Channel coast, include hand-painted shop signs, above, streets of half-timbered and shuttered houses, left and above right, and a quiet port, right.

CHATEAU DE ROSANBO

One of Brittany's most handsome family-owned châteaux, the Château de Rosanbo, dominates the Bo valley a few miles inland from the Côte de Granite Rose. The Breton name *Rosanbo* means, literally, "rock on the Bo." The Coskaer de Rosanbos are descendants of an ancient Breton clan who built a fortified castle on a rocky promontory overlooking the Bo River valley in 1050. The castle that stands today was constructed in the 14th century, partially redesigned in the 17th, and, finally, completely restored in the 19th. Bordered by elegant terraced gardens and esplanades designed by André Le Nôtre, the landscape architect of Versailles, and surrounded by almost five miles of woodland trails, the château enjoys an aristocratic setting unusual even for France.

A graceful pool installed in the 17th century reflects the mottled image of the Château de Rosanbo, a historic residence that has remained in the same family since the 11th century. A stone urn filled with geraniums, below, is one of many architectural ornaments embellishing the property.

The crestlike design above the château's arched central doorway is repeated in the design of the reflecting pool it faces, left. One of the château's many *charmilles,* or *allées* planted with *charmes* (hornbeam trees), right, leads out of the gardens and into the woods.

A MANOIR IN MORLAIX

When Jacques and Colette (Coco) LeBour bought their 17th-century manor house, it was little more than a ramshackle farm. A family of four lived in the dining room, and animals everywhere else. Set in the bucolic farmland of northern Brittany a few miles southeast of Morlaix, the LeBour house was built at a time of great prosperity for the region. Like most of the fine houses in Brittany, it is constructed of hand-hewn granite and topped by a roof covered with the hand-cut slate tiles that are characteristic of traditional Breton architecture.

Bringing the manoir back to its original state required years of work. Breton-born Jacques, a businessman in Morlaix, and

The LeBour family, left—Colette (Coco) and Jacques, with daughters Youna and Gaëlle—gathers in front of their restored manor house with an assortment of resident animals. Their garden, some of which is glimpsed against the manor wall, includes the typical Breton combination of hydrangeas and climbing roses.

Coco, a superb cook originally from Provence, slowly restored the house and grounds over more than a decade, supplementing old beams with new, enlarging rooms, replacing roses cut down by the previous tenants, and planting masses of hydrangeas. Daughters Gaëlle and Youna participated as color consultants. The manor today, a well-groomed homestead with an atmosphere of radiant warmth, has, as Coco describes it, a certain "sweet disorder," all the better she believes for living and loving comfortably.

The extensive grounds include a large *grange*, or barn, marked for future renovation, an enchanting courtyard garden, and a large, flourishing *potager*, or vegetable garden, just beyond the kitchen door. Domestic animals still share the property, but today only a cat and a dog reside, occasionally, indoors. Outside, turkeys strut along the garden paths, while hens shelter their chicks beside sun-warmed rocks.

Coco LeBour's philosophy of comfortable decorating emphasizes the usable antique. Here a quaint makeshift lampshade—a bit of antique lace tucked around an old frame—gives the living room a romantic glow of *temps perdu*.

In the rustic, heavily beamed family living room, left, a companionable array of comfortable armchairs clusters around the original 17th-century fireplace. Coco prefers her rooms "not impeccable," she says. "They are much more livable a bit *tordu*, just slightly askew." A large harvest table, here set in anticipation of luncheon for nine, dominates the generously proportioned dining room, below left. The embroidered tablecloth was hand-stitched for Coco's mother.

Youna's pink-patterned bedroom is petite and playful, just like its occupant. The wrought-iron bed is an early 20th-century *lit romantique*. "Every young girl at the turn of the century had one," says Youna.

The bedroom of Gaëlle, an art student, also functions as her atelier. She chose a soft butterscotch shade, a color neutral but warm, for both walls and curtains. Her bed is a rustic, turn-of-the-century *lit de coin* (corner bed).

oco's spacious farm-style kitchen is superbly functional, with broad tiled work areas, a full paneled wall of open shelving, and a large herb garden just outside the door. Baskets, pots, jars, and cooking implements are displayed on every surface.

104

"I find kitchen equipment very beautiful," says Coco, "and I like to see it all around me." An excellent cook, she enjoys entertaining frequently for family and friends.

At the weekly Saturday morning open market in the old town of Morlaix, Coco and Gaëlle fill their baskets with fruits, flowers, bread, and shellfish from Brittany's north coast. Here, as in virtually every other French town on market day, the occasion is social as well as practical.

After a morning of marketing, fresh purchases are laid out on a garden table outside the kitchen. In addition to the local fish (already stored in the refrigerator), flowers, onions, raspberries, and lettuce, the market basket includes wine from Bordeaux, cheese from Normandy, and melon from Provence.

FAR BRETON

- **3** large eggs
- **½** cup sugar
- **1** cup all-purpose flour
- **2** cups whole milk, at room temperature (see Note)
- **1** cup pitted dried prunes, dried apricots, or raisins soaked in brandy or fruit juice, or 1 cup pitted fresh cherries (optional)
- **2** ounces (½ stick) salted butter
  Salt

Preheat the oven to 400° F.

In a large bowl, beat the eggs lightly. Add the sugar and blend well. Add the flour and mix until smooth.

Add the milk little by little, mixing all the while to blend. Sprinkle in a pinch of salt and stir. If using the fruit, stir it into the batter, distributing it evenly.

Coat an oval ceramic baking dish approximately 12 × 7 × 1½ inches with a thick film of butter. Pour the batter into the baking dish and distribute it evenly over the bottom.

Bake 35 to 40 minutes, or until the top of the pudding is deeply browned. Serve slightly warm.

NOTE: *If desired, substitute 1½ cups whole milk blended with ½ cup heavy cream to approximate the rich milk of Brittany.*

Serves 6

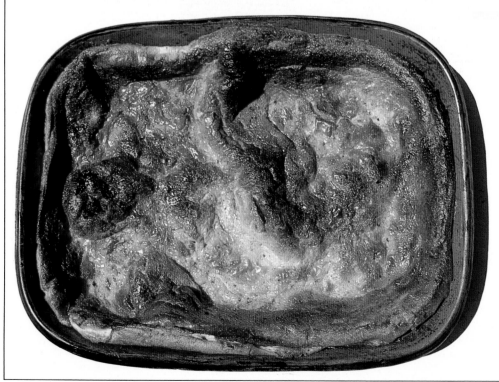

Taking advantage of a warm weekend afternoon, and leaving the kitchen free for Coco's dinner preparations, Youna and a visiting friend, Alexa, prepare *far breton*, a traditional sweet baked custard, in the garden. The finished product, left, has a distinctive brown crust.

The grounds of the home present as many charming vignettes as the interior: A mother hen and her chicks, left, enjoy a moment of calm atop an old stone drinking trough. Its roof recently restored, a large *grange*, or barn, above, presently used for storage, stands ready for future interior renovation. Roses, flowering vines, and hydrangeas, above right and far right, adorn the austere stone walls of the house, transforming a rather cold exterior into a bright and welcoming one. Doors and window frames are painted a soft gray-green, "to match the lichen on the stone," says Coco. The nearby well, right, with the same slate roof and granite walls as the house, is also skirted with roses.

LES ILES BRETONNES

The experience of being in Brittany is never so intense as it is on one of the innumerable islands that are strung along the coast like a long strand of rough-cut gems.

The isolation that pervades the character of any island is compounded in the Breton islands by the old-fashioned aspect of much of the province; these *îles* seem like microcosms lost in time and lost at sea. Of the larger and more distinctive islands, there are Bréhat and the Ile de Batz in the Channel; Ouessant and Molène in the waters off northern Finistère; Groix and the Glénan Islands in southern Finistère; and Belle-Ile, Houat, Hoëdic, and the Iles du Morbihan in the waters of Brittany's deep south. Each of these islands has its own personality—cheerful and warm, gentle and reserved, sunny but austere, savage but intriguing.

No contrast between island personalities is more dramatic than that between Ouessant in the north of Brittany and the Iles du Morbihan in the south. Tied to the same province, set in

the same ocean and, geologists affirm, all once a part of the mainland in an earlier age, Ouessant and the Morbihan Islands nevertheless have so little in common they hardly seem to be part of the same country, or even the same time.

Traveling to the island of Ouessant is a voyage to the core of a place and a people, Brittany in its essence—tough, fierce, isolated, and fervently religious. It is, as the French say, *la France profonde*—deep France. Ouessant, thirteen miles out in the open sea due west from Brest, is a place of stark reality that makes concessions to no one and nothing but the sea. *Qui voit Ouessant voit son sang* ("He who sees Ouessant sees his blood") goes the old seafarer's dictum, alluding to the infamous dangers of the island waters spiked with treacherous black reefs. Overwhelming in its simplicity and its solitude, Ouessant appeals most to those with a taste for the ends of the earth.

For centuries Ouessant had an almost mythic reputation. Dominated by grim, black-garbed, white-coiffed women whose husbands and sons spent as many as seven consecutive years at sea, it was perceived as an island of "howling priestesses," violent winter winds, and shipwrecks. A shroud of fog wraps the island for more than forty days a year, augmenting the isolation with total inaccessibility. Ouessant, *Ile de l'épouvante* ("Island of Dread"), sailors called it. Spiritual

vestiges of the Druids, who once inhabited the island and believed it to be the kingdom closest to the gods, seem to remain in the air.

A world away from Ouessant in spirit, and about 150 miles south in actual distance, are the Iles du Morbihan, islands that bathe in the temperate coastal waters of the Morbihan *département* off shore from Quiberon, Auray, and Vannes. Belle-Ile, Moines, Houat, Hoëdic, and Groix are among the hundreds of small islands, some hardly larger than a camel's hump, that enjoy the gentle tides, soft breezes, and meridional climate that blesses the Morbihan, which means "little sea" in Breton. Within the Golfe du Morbihan, an island sea embraced by the curving arm of the Rhuys Peninsula, there is said to be an island for every day of the year. Caesar and Brutus cruised these waters in their oar-powered galleys, challenging and eventually conquering the Gauls in the middle of the 1st century B.C.

The craggy, massive boulders that spike the waters around Ouessant, left, make it one of the most difficult islands to reach in Europe, especially in waters as rough as those depicted in the 19th-century painting, above. A world away in temperament is the Ile aux Moines, where the small cheerful restaurant Chez Charlemagne, right, serves a variety of simple menus.

OUESSANT

Ouessant has one small village, Lampaul, with about 1,200 inhabitants and a few amenities for tourists. Beyond the *bourg* of Lampaul, however, the island—four miles long and two and one half miles wide—is decidedly more *sauvage* than civilized. The landscape ranges from undulating heaths awash with blossoms to ravaged, sinister cliffs. The northwest coast, with its haunting legions of jagged rocks in high relief against the sky, is the island's most dramatic side. Farther west, past the blazing pink and yellow fields of heather, gorse, and broom, stands the Créac'h lighthouse. A looming tower painted in bold black and white bands, Le Créac'h is one of the most powerful lighthouses in the world, with 16 million candlepower and an average range of about thirty-seven miles. Beyond Le Créac'h lies the Pointe de Pern, a humbling cluster of looming reefs that resembles the crenellated ruins of a medieval fortress.

The boat trip to Ouessant, left, is rarely gentle. Those who embark from the port of Brest for this outermost island should be prepared for a journey of two to three hours through an often churlish and sometimes wild sea. Dramatic bands of black and white distinguish Ouessant's Le Créac'h Lighthouse, one of the most powerful in the world.

The most visible natives of Ouessant are the flocks of sheep that graze on the grassy plains that stretch across the island. The baby lambs remain free while the mothers are tethered to unusual three-sided, star-shaped shelters that give protection from the wind, no matter in which direction it blows. Although typical of the local sheep, this family is unusual in one way: there are three lambs instead of the usual two.

On the northeast part of the island, built on the Pointe de Bac'haol, is the handsome hewn-granite Stiff lighthouse, whose tower was built in 1695. Designed by the military engineer Sébastien Le Prestre de Vauban, Stiff is one of the oldest lighthouses in France still in service. Every lighthouse has its unique signal and color, explains Michel Berthèle, Stiff's keeper. Stiff flashes its red light twice every twenty seconds, broadcasting the message: "isolated and dangerous."

Open to the world with daily boat service from Brest and even air service in clement weather, Ouessant still feels like a place

Ouessant's crack sea-rescue team, part of France's national Société Nautique de Sauvetage en Mer, or SNSM, meets every Saturday for rescue drills and equipment checks. The organization is manned solely by volunteers and funded by donations. Of the sixty-nine sea-rescue stations in Brittany, the teams on the islands of Ouessant, Molène, and Sein are particularly renowned for their cour-

age and seafaring skills. Current team members, above, are posed before their day on the water. Clockwise from top left are Jean-Jacques Gonin, Michel LeGall, Michel Louet, Jean Rolland, Victor Guermeur, Joseph Grunweiser, and Antoine Noret.

apart. Its name in Breton—*Enez Eussa* (the Most Distant Island)—is apt. Ouessant is the westernmost outpost of continental Europe. Electricity did not light Ouessant's nights until 1951, and television arrived only in 1962.

In parts, Ouessant looks like a ghost town. But there are also small neighborhoods of sturdy, neatly kept granite houses, painted white or left unadorned. Here and there, isolated on bluffs on the island, are a handful of large, even grandiose houses whose exposure to bitter winds is compensated for by panoramic views and total privacy. The only vivid color on the island, aside from the local flora, is provided by the trim on the shutters, doors, and gates of both large and small homes, usually a rich Breton blue or occasionally a deep green. No garish hues detract from the blue-to-slate-to-gunmetal of the big sky, the soft rainbow of colors on the heaths, or the mottled, inky hues of the sea.

For more than a hundred years, each rescue mission undertaken by the Ouessant Sauvetage en Mer team has been permanently recorded on a plaque installed in the boathouse. Rescue efforts noted on the plaque for the mid-1970s, right, include a search for a downed plane, picking up a sick crew member from a Polish cargo ship, and saving the passengers and crew from several yachts that foundered on the island's treacherous rocks.

Canot Patron Fçois Morin (suite)

SORTIES	DATES			CIRCONSTANCES
174	9	10	69	BATEAU de pêche du CONQUET pas rentré
175	3	1	70	RECHERCHE d'un AVION tombé à la mer
176	3	7	70	BATEAU de pêche "A DIEUVAT" échoué au GOUBARS
177	26	7	70	YACHT "DURACUIR II" Remorqué à BREST
178	11	8	70	"KOMETA" échoué au STIFF
179	18	8	70	YACHT "Reder Mor II" en diff.té aux PIERRES-VERTES
180	18	12	70	BLESSE sur le Chalutier "Ste Anne d'AURAY"
181	9	4	71	Canot de Sau tage "DUGUAY-TROUIN"
182	14	7	71	CHERCHER un nageur parti d'ARLAN
183	16	8	71	BATEAU de pêche "BLEIZ Ar MOR" en difficulté
184	26	12	71	YACHT SUEDOIS "SYSLA II" en détresse
185	21	5	72	YACHT "PEGUEMENN" en difficulté
186	12	6	72	MALADE sur CARGO POLONAIS
187	29	6	72	CARGO BRESILIEN en difficulté
188	7	9	72	MALADE sur CARGO GREC
189	10	10	72	BLESSE sur PETROLIER ANGLAIS
190	13	10	72	Chalutier "ATALANDE" en dérive
191	15	1	73	YACHT ANGLAIS "FREEMAD" en détresse
192	15	2	73	DYNGHY au LARGE de KELLER
193	17	5	73	BATEAU de pêche "BLEIZ AR MOR" en difficulté
194	19	5	73	YACHT ROYAL HOLLANDAIS en détresse
195	11	6	73	PLATE en DERIVE
196	4	2	74	Chalutier "SANTA HELENA" en difficulté
197	21	3	74	CANOT en DERIVE
198	25	5	74	BATEAU "L'AMOUR du MARIN" en difficulté
199	20	7	74	BATEAU de pêche "LE KERUEL" pas rentré au port
200	21	7	74	PLATE Chavirée à PEN AR ROCH
201	23	8	74	CANOT de pêche "MARIE" pas rentré au port
202	25	8	74	FUSEES rouges près de KELLER
203	22	11	74	YACHT échoué sur les rochers de LAMPAUL
204	1	12	74	PETROLIER Grec "KEF EAGLE" en panne de moteur
205	28	6	75	YACHT "EXONIDORE" en difficulté
206	2	8	75	BATEAU de pêche "PETITE SIMONE" pas rentré au port
207	6	8	75	YACHT "DAOU" en difficulté
208	18	8	75	YACHT "RIDENDO" abordé par P.E.T.ier PANAMEEN
209	9	9	75	YACHT LUXEMBOURGEOIS "MELUSINA II" en diff.tés
210	11	9	75	Caboteur NORVEGIEN "OEYTRADER" 6 HOMMES sauvés
211	15	9	75	Chalutier "NEIZ-BIHAN" en panne de moteur
212	1	11	75	CARGO ALLEMAND "MATHIAS REITH" panne de moteur
213	28	12	75	YACHT "BLEIZ DU" en difficulté

LIVING BRETON MUSEUM

The *ecomusée*, in the hamlet of Niou-Huella, an intriguing museum of island life and traditions, has recently been refurbished. Arranged in two restored stone cottages, one decorated as a peasant's home the way it would have been in 1866, the *ecomusée* offers a glimpse back into Ouessantine history, with its collections of domestic objects, nautical memorabilia, and costumes. The blue-and-white-painted furniture that decorates the house was created, as all island furniture once was, from wood salvaged from shipwrecks.

The Ouessant home of Victor Guermeur, a recently retired career navy man who is an active member of the Ouessant sea-rescue team, is almost a time capsule of the turn-of-the-century bourgeois island home. The traditional blue-and-white painted furniture includes an old grandfather clock, above, *vaisseliers* (dishracks) and display cases for religious *objets*, above right, and a *lit clos*, right.

123

ILES DU MORBIHAN

Sheltered from the open sea by a large peninsula, some of the islands in the Morbihan gulf have grown lush. On Moines, just a mile and a half from the mainland and the largest of the archipelago, the heady scents of mimosas, camellias, and roses mingle with the gentle fragrances of lemon and orange trees. Along the island's narrow *ruelles* (or tiny streets), masses of hydrangeas soften the granite facades of small *chaumières* (thatched-roof cottages) that are as beguiling as dollhouses. Here, the poetic names of thickly wooded glens hint at a history of romantic island trysts: the Bois des Soupirs (the Wood of Sighs); the Bois d'Amour (the Wood of Love); and the Bois des Regrets (the Wood of Regrets). As befits this sunny and cheerful *île*, the traditional woman's costume is lavishly embroidered with bright flowers and crowned with a low white lace *coiffe* also worked in floral motifs. Many visitors arrive for a taste of the gentle life on Moines, disembarking in the small sunny port, where pleasure boats, ferries, and commercial fishing vessels converge. The vast seasonal appeal of the island expands its population tenfold, from about 500 to 5,000, between April and early September.

The sun-bathed white-washed cottages of the Ile aux Moines are bordered by an assortment of flowers in a merry kaleidoscope of colors that thrive in the balmy climate of the Gulf Stream. In contrast to the riot of bright flora, the generally small houses of the island, painted white or left as natural stone, are daubed with color only on shutters and doorways.

F lowers bank the pathways and narrow *ruelles*, or tiny roads, that wind up, down, and around the island. Among the most prevalent colors are rich butter yellow and vivid reds.

M any of the beguiling island homes on the Ile aux Moines are *chaumières*— thatched-roof cottages—such as the house, top, bordered by a neat stone wall, and the diminutive 18th-century granite cottage, above, fronted by two massive hydrangea bushes.

THE CORSAIR'S ISLAND REFUGE

At the tip of one of the small Morbi-han islands sits a handsome, 17th-century granite mansion protected by high stone walls. (The current owners' desire for privacy pro-scribes identifying the island precisely.) The house was built in 1633 by a wealthy corsair, or privateer, who erected the walls so he did not have to look at the sea when he was home between voyages. Today the seventh generation of a well-known literary family resides in the house, continuing a tradition of more than one hundred years. The owners live on their little island throughout the year, welcoming children

The front facade of this 17th-century island man-sion is lavishly covered with wisteria vines that transform the home into a vision of lav-ender-blue in early summer. Red, white, and blue is the home's color theme, chosen to harmonize with the blue-and-white 18th-century Delft tiles that adorn the elegant living room, right. Gracefully carved *boiserie*, or wainscot-ing, dating from the 18th cen-tury enhances this spacious and luminous salon.

and grandchildren during school holidays and summer vacations.

The twelve rooms of the house are furnished with armoires, beds, tables, and chairs "that have always been there," according to the owners. The lady of the house, however, has modernized the interior, creating a luminous, contemporary summer dining room with blue-and-white tile floors, walls of built-in bookshelves, and a striking glass dining table trimmed in deep blue, especially designed for the house. Accents of red, pink, and blue contrast with white walls and white woodwork throughout the house. The color scheme was chosen to harmonize with the blue-and-white Delft tiles that trim the living room walls, and with masses of blooming wisteria that cling to, and almost totally obscure, the front facade in early summer.

French doors bordered by antique Delft tiles open onto a shady terrace, left. The 18th-century *commode* holds a single vase of cut roses from the garden. Lush greenery, above, shelters the house from the world beyond, as does a high stone wall that blocks all views of the sea.

An armoire, above, holds glassware, linens, faïence, and tureens. Two large *armoires bretonnes*, right, flank the doorway into the kitchen, where a long farm table accommodates three generations of a large family.

A luminous summer dining room, left, which separates the living room and the kitchen, is fitted out as a library to accommodate some of the family's extensive book collection. The blue-trimmed glass dining table was created for the room by Paris designer Pierre Sala. On the half-floor landing between the first and second floors, above, two 17th-century carved wooden doors found in an attic have been adapted to enclose the facing built-in hall closets.

A rare set of early 19th-century Quimper faience plates and tureens is set out on the terrace for a luncheon buffet.

A small doorway in the high stone wall leads into the old corsair's retreat.

PONT-AVEN

Towering trees, mossy boulders, glens blanketed with pine needles, and the perpetually swirling Aven River beguile contemporary visitors to Pont-Aven, who come to stroll in the footsteps of the Post-Impressionists.

The modest river town of Pont-Aven, a few miles inland from the coast of southern Brittany near Concarneau, reveals little of its sophistication or history upon first encounter. What *is* striking about this graceful community of almost 4,000 residents, bisected by the gently flowing Aven River, is its neatness and quiet charm. The main street is lined with pristine galleries, boutiques, and antiques shops, some trellised with climbing roses around their doorways. Sculpted stonework adorns the facades of the three- and four-story houses on the main *place,* while peaked dormer windows set into the slate-tiled roofs enhance the town's low skyline. In the early morning or after sunset, hours when the sidewalks are clear of the flocks of midday visitors, the Aven, softly burbling as it passes through an ancient

waterwheel on its way to a tidal estuary, sounds a tranquilizing undertone.

Pont-Aven draws its many French and foreign tourists with its historic legacy as a once-important artistic community of Post-Impressionists, a group which came to be known as the Pont-Aven School. Enticed by the region's reputation as a haven with a mystical atmosphere and primeval beauty, the painter Paul Gauguin arrived in Pont-Aven in June 1886, forsaking his home and family in Paris for the Gloanec *pension* in the center of town. He was soon bewitched by the region's powerful Celtic spirit and forceful, untamed landscapes. "I love Brittany," he wrote at the time in his *Notebook for Aline*, the diary he kept for his daughter. "Here I've found the primitive wilderness. When my *sabots* echo on the granite, I hear the dull and mighty muted sounds that I seek in my canvases."

Shortly after his arrival in Brittany, Gauguin invited a group of dynamic young Post-Impressionists to come and paint with him in Pont-Aven. Among the artists who gathered around Gauguin, and eventually formed the Pont-Aven School of painters, were Emile Ber-

One of the most enchanting houses seen in the Pont-Aven environs is a small *chaumière*, or thatched-roof cottage, right, set on a corner in the small village of Riec-sur-Belon. The cottage, with its thick straw roof and flower-filled yard, has frequently won a local competition for the prettiest *maison fleurie*, literally "enflowered house." The sunset painting, above, courtesy of the Galerie Le Paul in Pont-Aven, which specializes in art of the Pont-Aven school, is the work of luminist Ferdinand du Puigadeau (1864–1930).

nard, Paul Sérusier, Maurice Denis, Charles Filiger, and Maxime-Louis Maufra. These avant-garde artists had begun to abandon the delicate techniques of the Impressionists, turning instead to a bolder, more geometric, primitive, and almost abstract style of painting that is very close in spirit, approach, and use of color to the modern movements of the 20th century. Inspired by the barren landscapes, and enjoying themselves immensely at the *pension* run by the *sympathique* Marie-Jeanne Gloanec, the artists spent several fruitful seasons in Pont-Aven before moving on to the nearby port town of Le Pouldu, and finally disbanding after 1896.

Many paintings of and by the Pont-Aven School are set in the Bois d'Amour—a romantic and mysterious copse that runs along the town's riverbank and then rises into the hills at its northern edge. The Bois d'Amour—its name referred to the nocturnal trysts that once took place on its banks and in its bowers—has haunted and inspired painters for more than one hundred years. Isolated, serene, and silent, the Bois d'Amour today has changed very little from the way it was when Gauguin and his colleagues meandered there a century ago.

The country lanes that wind around the Pont-Aven center lead to the nearby communities of Kerdruc, Rosbras, Port-Manech, Kerascoët, Belon, and Riec-sur-Belon. These tiny ports and villages dotting the countryside near the coast are ideal spots for a morning or afternoon sortie, to be followed by a leisurely lunch or dinner at Chez Melanie in Riec-sur-Belon for a succulent four- or five-course meal, at Chez Jacky's in Belon for the oysters that bear the town's name, or perhaps simply for a crêpe at Ty Couz in Riec-sur-Belon. The smallest roads on the map, or perhaps not even on the map, crisscross lovely fields of gorse and pass small *chaumières* and antique watermills.

Pont-Aven, once an unprepossessing mill town (fourteen working mills in the days of Gauguin), is today the center of a community of sophisticated residents, many originally from Paris and still active in the international art world. During the fall and winter, the hardy perennials left in town might cross paths buying croissants at the Boulangerie Kersale or fetching out-of-town newspapers at the Maison de la Presse, once Marie-Jeanne Gloanec's popular *pension*.

Trellised roses border a discreetly marked antiques shop on a side street in Pont-Aven, left. One of the most popular stops in the center of Pont-Aven is the Traou Mad cookie shop, right, which sells a variety of traditional Breton butter cookies prepared at a small local factory. The coiffed ladies in the painting, above, in the collection of Pont-Aven's Galerie Le Paul, were painted by Pegot Ogier (1877–1915), a member of Gauguin's circle of painters.

Scented geraniums and fuchsia fill an unusual 19th-century sculpted urn, left, on the grounds of a château near Pont-Aven. After lunch, a foursome plays a game of *boules*, above, a popular pastime throughout France. The window of the Galeries de Pont-Aven, above right, displays a cornucopia of locally produced comestibles, including cookies, vinegars, honey, and crêpes. Flowers threaten to obscure the view from a window of a home in Pont-Aven, right. Even the men's open-air *pissoir* over the Pont-Aven River, far right, has a piquant charm, with its precise, miniaturized architectural detailing in granite and slate.

A VISIT TO TREMALO

The chapel of Trémalo, set on the edge of broad fields on a hill above Pont-Aven, is a treasure often over- looked by many tourists. Built of granite blocks more than 300 years ago, this Breton country chapel has an un- usual asymmetrical roofline: one eave slopes almost to the ground. Inside is the carved 16th-century polychrome Christ that was the inspiration for Gauguin's *Yellow Christ*. (Gauguin removed the crucifix from the chapel and set it in a nearby field, sur- rounded by figures of praying women.) In addition to the crucifix, there is a startling collection of naïve polychrome grotesques carved into the massive roof beams that run the chapel's length and breadth. These whimsical figures, created by local carpen- ters, are intended to remind the devout of the sins they are to avoid.

The Trémalo Chapel, left, set on a hill overlooking the town of Pont-Aven, was constructed in the 16th cen- tury by local stonemasons and carpenters. Gauguin used the 16th-century carved Christ, right, as the model for his *Yellow Christ*.

Among the most striking examples of old Breton folk art are the imaginative figures along the beams of the Trémalo Chapel carved by local carpenters of the 17th and 18th centuries. These small polychrome grotesques, ironic and humorous as much as they are cautionary, depict the sins of gluttony, pride, and avarice in many guises.

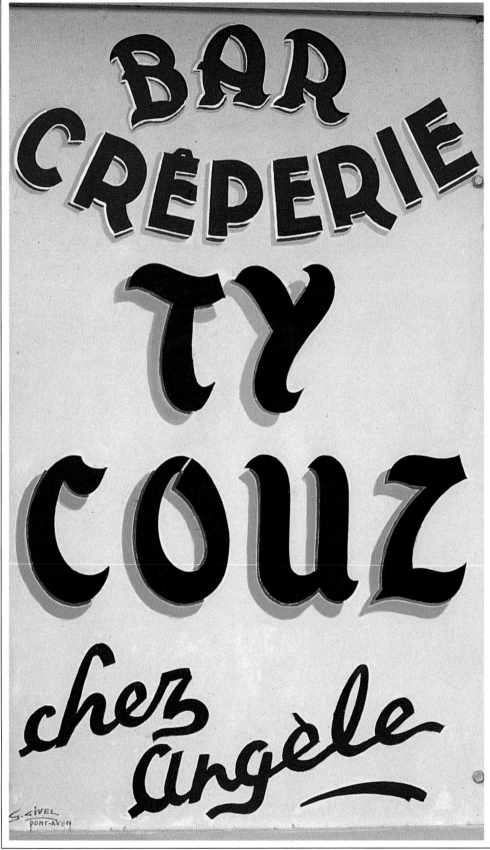

CHEZ ANGELE

In the village of Riec-sur-Belon, a few minutes' drive from the historic town of Pont-Aven, Marie-Renée Offret tends the *galétoire* (the crêpe iron) as well as the little bar of the thatched-roof Crêperie Ty Couz, also called La Chaumière de Chez Angèle. Here, surrounded by a simple, appealing decor of fresh flowers and old Breton furniture, one can feast on crêpes starting at about four francs for a *crêpe au sucre,* or sugar crêpe. The ultimate crêpe, a *crêpe aux bananes flambés,* a banana crêpe flambéed in Grand Marnier, sells for about fourteen francs. Marie-Renée, the daughter of the founder, Angèle, melts a large pat of butter on the *galétoire,* ladles about half a cupful of thin batter over the hot surface, and then quickly spreads it out with a small wooden paddle. In less than two minutes she flips the delicate crêpe with a spatula, spoons on the filling, and then folds the edges to make a square envelope. Finally, she deftly slides the crêpe onto a plate and serves it immediately. Enjoyed with a bottle of sparkling cider from a nearby farm, the crêpe is a perfect light meal in a small package.

At the Crêperie Ty Couz (Chez Angèle), Marie-Renée Offret offers crêpes with a wide variety of fillings, including sausage, eggs, ratatouille, mushrooms, and ham and cheese.

148

Rough granite walls and antique carved Breton furniture complement a table set with sparkling cider, butter, jam, and two of Marie-Renée's buckwheat crêpes. Marie-Renée, below, prepares her delicate crêpes in the rustic ambience of the old establishment founded by her mother in Riec-sur-Belon.

THE ULTIMATE FRUITS DE MER

For those who truly love oysters, the tiny port of Belon is mecca. This is where the great *belon* oysters are raised in hundreds of flat "beds" scattered along the mouth of the Belon River. Washed by salt water as the tide comes in, and by fresh water as the tide flows out, the flat, disklike oysters have a unique, clean, delicately iodized flavor. To eat true *belons* in Paris is already an exquisite pleasure. To eat *belons* by the Belon River, seated a few feet above the very beds where they are growing, is an almost religious experience.

The small port of Belon, top, just upriver from where the Belon River meets the Atlantic, is lively with small fishing and pleasure craft. Low tide exposes the oyster beds that rest just under the water near the riverbanks, above. Chez Jacky, right, is the only restaurant in the port. (Photo: Linda Dannenberg)

150

A young couple, top left, gazes out at the placid harbor scene, top right, on an early summer morning. A boy, above, dressed in a classic Breton fisherman's jersey, docks his inflatable boat after a sortie into the harbor. A superb *plateau de fruits de mer* (seafood platter), prepared at Jacky's and set on the restaurant's deck, left, includes three kinds of oysters, crabs, langoustines, shrimp, clams, and periwinkles.

LE MOULIN DE ROSMADEC

Old weeping willows and banks of deep pink geraniums border the Aven River where it flows by the Moulin de Rosmadec, a romantic restaurant sequestered in a small courtyard behind Pont-Aven's main thoroughfare. Although this 15th-century mill has long ceased grinding grain, its waterwheel still turns, making an idyllic setting even more serene. One of the finest restaurants in Brittany—meriting one Michelin star (and, in the opinion of many, on the verge of a second)—the Moulin de Rosmadec, now in its second decade of operation, is run with quiet pride and a master's touch by chef-owner Pierre Sebilleau and his wife, Gabrielle.

Within the restaurant, light filters through antique mullioned windows across tables laid with pink linens. Thick dark beams traverse the ceiling, and a stone fireplace piled with kindling stands ready to warm the dining room on chilly days. Antique Breton cupboards displaying local faience and turn-of-the-century tableaux featuring barefoot Breton maids complete the welcoming ambience.

A narrow *ruelle* leads to the romantic entrance of the Moulin de Rosmadec, left, hidden among the willows along the Aven River's banks behind Pont-Aven's main square. Chef Pierre Sebilleau and his wife, Gabrielle, far right, opened their restaurant in the mid-1970s.

HUITRES FARCIES AUX AMANDES

Stuffed Oysters with Almonds

Coarse salt (enough to make a bed for the oysters)
2 dozen fresh oysters
2 ounces slivered almonds

STUFFING

8 ounces (2 sticks) lightly salted butter, at room temperature
2 shallots, minced
1 small garlic clove, minced
⅓ cup minced fresh parsley
Freshly ground pepper

Butter for dotting

Preheat the oven to 450° F.

Spread a bed of coarse salt in the bottom of a baking pan with a rim. Loosen the oysters in the half shells, then carefully arrange the half shells in the salt so that they do not tip over.

For the stuffing, combine the butter, shallots, garlic, parsley, and pepper and mix thoroughly. Place a spoonful of stuffing over each oyster, then sprinkle them with slivered almonds and dot with butter.

Bake the oysters until the almonds are golden brown, about 2 minutes.

Serves 4

Moulin de Rosmadec's incomparable *huîtres farcies aux amandes* arrive in a group of six on a bed of seaweed. As soon as the first six are consumed, another half-dozen arrive still bubbling from the broiler.

SALADE DE LANGOUSTE

Rock Lobster Salad

- 1 rock lobster tail (about 1¼ to 1½ pounds)
  Salt
- ¼ pound salad greens (mâche, if possible)

VINAIGRETTE

- 1 shallot, minced
- 1 tablespoon wine vinegar
- 3 tablespoons vegetable oil
  Salt
  Freshly ground pepper

MAYONNAISE

- 1 egg, separated
- 1 teaspoon mustard
- ½ cup vegetable oil
- 1 teaspoon freshly squeezed lemon juice
  Salt
  Freshly ground pepper

GARNISH

- 1 tomato

Bring 1 quart water plus 1 tablespoon salt to a boil in a large pot. Add the rock lobster tail, cover, and steam the lobster over medium heat 12 minutes.

Drain the lobster tail and cool under cold running water. Shell the lobster tail in one piece, then slice the meat crosswise into ½-inch-thick slices.

While the lobster tail is cooking, prepare the two sauces and the tomato garnish.

For the vinaigrette: combine the shallot, vinegar, and oil. Season to taste with salt and pepper.

For the mayonnaise: Combine the egg yolk and mustard, and whisk thoroughly. Slowly drizzle the oil into the egg mixture a few drops at a time, whisking until the mayonnaise is thick. Season to taste with lemon juice,

salt, and pepper. Beat the egg white until stiff and fold into the mayonnaise.

For the garnish: Peel the tomato, then quarter it and remove the inside pulp. Dice the tomato flesh.

Toss the salad greens with the vinaigrette. Taste and adjust seasoning. Divide the greens between each plate. Dip each medallion of lobster into the mayonnaise and decorate the greens with the medallions. Decorate the tops of the medallions with diced tomato.

Serves 2

The bright and succulent langouste salad created from local rock lobster is one of the Moulin de Rosmadec's most popular appetizers.

DOS DE SAUMON AU GROS SEL

Poached Salmon with Coarse Salt

¼ cup finely minced shallots (about 4 shallots)
  Salt
1 cup dry white wine
1 1½-pound salmon fillet, with skin
1 large fresh tomato
  Few drops freshly squeezed lemon juice
6 ounces (1½ sticks) unsalted butter
  Pepper
2 tablespoons olive oil

GARNISH

Coarse salt

Place the shallots in a small stainless-steel saucepan with ⅓ cup water, a pinch of salt, and the wine. Cover tightly and cook over low heat until the shallots are very tender but not browned, about 10 minutes. Uncover, and reduce the shallots over high heat to 1 tablespoon. Set aside.

Meanwhile, cut the salmon fillet crosswise into 4 pieces. Bring 1 quart water to a boil in a fish poacher or a 6-quart ovenproof casserole dish. Place the fish on a rack that fits into the poacher or

casserole, and set over the boiling water. Cover and steam the salmon until done, about 10 minutes. (Insert a toothpick in the flesh of the salmon to test; if it gives no resistance, the fish is ready.)

Meanwhile, place the tomato in a small pan of boiling water for 30 seconds, then transfer it to a bowl of cold water. Drain the tomato and peel it. Quarter the tomato and remove the pulp, leaving only the flesh. Dice

the tomato flesh and season it to taste with salt and lemon juice. Reserve.

Cut the butter into small pieces and add it to the shallot reduction over very low heat. Add the tomato and whisk until well blended. Season with salt and pepper, then drizzle in the olive oil, whisking constantly.

Ladle the sauce onto the plates, then place the fish skin side up on top of the sauce. Decorate the salmon with a few grains of coarse salt and serve.

Serves 4

Another vivid and appealing choice from Chef Sebilleau is the *saumon au gros sel*, accompanied here by a local muscadet, a white wine produced just across the Breton border in the Loire Valley and adopted by Brittany as its regional wine.

CREPES SUZETTE

CREPES

- 2 cups all-purpose flour
- 4 large eggs
- 2 cups milk
- 2 ounces (½ stick) unsalted butter, melted, plus additional for cooking
- 1½ teaspoons olive oil

SYRUP

- 4 oranges
- 3 tablespoons unsalted butter
- 3 tablespoons sugar
- 2 tablespoons Curaçao
- 1 tablespoon Cointreau

- 1 tablespoon sugar
- 2 tablespoons Cognac
- 2 tablespoons Grand Marnier

Sift the flour into a large mixing bowl. Make a well in the flour and break in the eggs. Beat the eggs lightly in the well, then whisk in the milk, combining gradually with the flour. (Work from the center toward the edges of the bowl.)

Stir in the melted butter and the oil. Pour the batter into a food processor and process 5 seconds, or until the batter is smooth. Let stand 30 minutes. Pour the batter through a sieve to strain out any remaining lumps.

Brush butter inside 7-inch crêpe pans (the process is faster if you have several pans on hand). Tilt each pan and pour in just enough batter to spread evenly over the bottom. Cook each crêpe until the underside is light golden brown. Using a long, flexible steel spatula, flip crêpes over and continue cooking until golden, about 3 minutes.

For the syrup: Cut strips of orange rind from one orange with a vegetable peeler, and cut the strips into fine julienne. Juice all the oranges (you should have about 1½ cups juice).

In a large skillet, combine the orange juice, butter, sugar, Curaçao, and Cointreau. Place the skillet over high heat and when the syrup is just short of boiling, carefully add the crêpes to the syrup. When soaked, remove the crêpes to a preheated platter, folding them in half twice to form a wedge.

Bring the remaining syrup to a boil and cook until it thickens slightly. Pour over the crêpes and sprinkle with 1 tablespoon sugar.

To flambé the crêpes using a gas range: Pour the Cognac into a ladle and hold it over the flame. When the liqueur is hot, tilt the ladle so that it catches fire in the flame and pour over the crêpes. Repeat with the Grand Marnier and serve immediately.

To flambé using an electric range: Heat the liqueurs one at a time in a small saucepan. When each liqueur is hot, remove the pan from the stove, ignite the liqueur with a match, and pour over crêpes.

Makes about 22 7-inch crêpes
Serves 6

Crêpes Suzette, bathed in an orange liqueur sauce, are flambéed for diners at their tables. A well-known and traditional dish served all over France, crêpes Suzette are seldom prepared so exquisitely as they are at this one-star restaurant.

elegant *oeil-de-boeuf* (bull's-eye) window and delicate wrought-iron window railings. But the house's real treasure can be found inside, where a collection of 19th-century naturalist murals, many in the form of medallions, adorns the walls of the foyer and dining room. An unusual feature for a French home, these paintings were commissioned by the owners from an itinerant artist to depict scenes of the environs.

The couple who inherited the château originally used it only on holidays and in the summer but now live here year round. The château's liveliest season is still the summer—true for much of coastal Brittany—when children and grandchildren, babysitters, and friends descend on this sheltered, well-sited home for a month or two of salt air, incomparable views, and a long stretch of family togetherness.

A rare—perhaps unique—set of medallionlike wall paintings, left, below, and opposite, created about 1870 by an itinerant artist, embellishes the walls of the foyer and dining room.

Old French metal park chairs, lacquered white, left, are placed casually around the property in warm weather, imparting a summer-house air. A small dormer window in the center of the château's roof, above, brings light and air to an attic room.

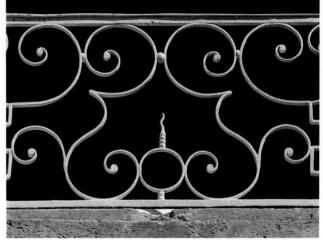

Children and grandchildren on a summer visit to the château gather for a story session on a garden bench, top. Graceful wrought-iron grilles, above, protect windows and a balcony beyond the French doors on the second floor. The château's shutters, left, are painted a soft gray to harmonize with the stonework.

THE HARBOR HOUSE WITH AN AMERICAN SOUL

Overlooking one of the many small harbors that punctuate the coast of southern Brittany, this rambling 19th-century house—at one time a sailors' restaurant—is actually two houses attached to form a small compound. It was purchased and renovated several years ago by a vivacious American grande dame, originally from Philadelphia, who has spent most of her life in France, where she married a French art dealer and raised a family. The granite harbor house, acquired after the sale of an immense family château outside Paris, appealed because of its simplicity, cozy proportions, and private rural setting. The owner, now widowed, wanted a comfortable vacation retreat for herself, her children, and her grandchildren, and, although most of the rooms are full of French antiques, the keynote remains one of casual comfort.

As with many harbor or seaside Breton houses, windows, far left, are kept small to protect the interior from strong coastal winds. The American owner of the house, left, seated on her terrace, renounced a château in the Ile-de-France for this choice harborside perch in south Finistère. A view from the rear of the house, above right, reveals the rambling structure and spacious dimensions. The small cobbled courtyard, right, is hidden by the facade fronting the street.

To the passerby on the little road that de-scends to the harbor, the house presents an almost blank face. From the harbor, the view is little better. It is only within the small courtyard, and within the house it-self, that this discreet residence reveals its style and generous proportions. One large section is reserved for visiting children and grandchildren; there large, simply fur-nished rooms encourage playing and casual living *en famille*. In grandmother's domain, tranquility reigns. Collections assembled over a lifetime, such as a rare group of art deco decanters, are displayed to advantage on windowsills and fine regional antique ta-bles of all periods. Throughout the house, color is used with imagination and re-straint.

A wrought-iron candelabra, above, silhouetted at the open kitchen window, was purchased at the Marché aux Puces (Flea Market) in Paris. A collection of antique glass decanters, right, acquired during the 1930s, shows to advantage in front of a living room window.

The broad, low-ceilinged living room is furnished for comfort with a variety of upholstered sofas and armchairs. Backing a sofa, a cherry *table à tirette* (a table with a pull-out shelf) from the early 19th-century displays mementos and family photographs.

Flanking the doorway to the living room is a small 18th-century *garde-manger* trimmed with pewter hardware, in which food is kept behind pierced metal doors. Although some walls have been plastered and some, such as those in the foyer and the living room, have been left as natural stone, both surfaces provide a rough-textured backdrop for fine art and antiques.

A passageway from the foyer down to the kitchen connects two formerly separate houses. An electric bulb within an antique lantern illuminates the stairs. The painting is from the owner's collection of 20th-century landscapes, still lifes, and portraits.

A blue theme in the upstairs master bedroom is carried through from the painted beams and walls to the lampshade, the upholstery, and even the French primitive carved saint on the wall. The massive Breton canopy bed is hung with curtains that match the fabric of the Voltaire armchair in the window.

A gilded Louis XVI mirror in the master bedroom hangs above an early 19th-century walnut dresser laden with family portraits. The blue-on-white fabric covering the two armchairs is toile de Jouy.

ness in the air. Driving through the interior, one always expects the sea to appear over the next rise, but the patch of water one glimpses is more likely to be one of the rivers in a weblike system that provides the crucial link between the Argoat and the Armor, the Brittany of the forests and the Brittany of the sea.

Much of the landscape in the interior near Rennes is wild and remote. There are a handful of interesting historic feudal enclaves such as Josselin, Combourg, and Fougères that have impressive fortified castles dating from the Middle Ages. For the most part, though, the land is rugged, with an occasional small village or farm. Eighty-five miles west of Rennes is the ancient Brocéliande of Arthurian legend, today called the Forest of Paimpont. Once an enormous and densely wooded expanse, the current forest of Paimpont has been reduced by centuries of logging and clearing to less than a third of its original eighty-seven-mile territory. Diminished though it is, Paimpont still has the profound and eerie atmosphere of the forest primeval. In the fall, a scattering of deep pools and ponds reflects the golden leaves of the tall beech trees and the thick, squat silhouettes of the box hedges. The heady, sweet fragrance of heather and broom and

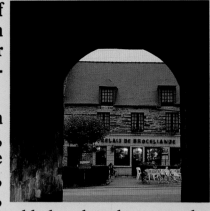

the rich, earthy smells of moist bark and fallen leaves perfume the air on warm autumn afternoons.

Several villages within the forest, or at its edge, such as Les Forges de Paimpont, Saint-Léry, Tréhorenteuc, Beignon, and Paimpont, itself, have old churches that reward a brief visit. In Tréhorenteuc, for example, a stained-glass window illustrates the Holy Grail, and a series of paintings portrays the Knights of the Round Table and the legend of the Valley of No Return, one of the forest's haunting, and perhaps haunted, spots. France's elite military academy, Saint-Cyr, also lies within the forest's boundaries.

Among the several legendary sites in the forest are Merlin's tomb, the Rock of False Lovers, and the Fountain of Youth.

Near the village of Commana, in the hilly Monts d'Arrée region about an hour north of Quimper, the arched granite doorway of a humble 17th-century cottage, left, still bears the central stone recalling the year of its construction. A *relais* (inn) welcomes visitors to the nearby forest of Paimpont, above right (Photo: Pierre Hussenot). Women work with old-fashioned scythes in fields outside Rennes (Photo: Daniel Gallon).

The imposing castle of Combourg, above, near Rennes was built by the Du Guesclin family in the 11th century and later was owned by the father of the famous Romantic writer Chateaubriand. At the Saturday market in Rennes, right, greens and freshly cut flowers compete for shoppers' attention. (Photos: Daniel Gallon)

RENNES

The handsome, historic city of Rennes is the traditional capital of Brittany. It is a city divided between old and new, between academic and industrial, marked by the path of the Vilaine River, which flows through the town from east to west. To the north of the river, in the heart of town, is Le Vieux Rennes (Old Rennes) with half-timbered houses lining medieval streets. Rue de la Psalette, curving around the Saint Pierre Cathedral, the shopping street rue de Pont-aux-Foulons, and the rue Saint-Georges are among the streets that are showcases of 16th- and 17th-century architecture. They are especially precious since they are among the handful of old streets that survived a disastrous fire in 1720 that destroyed a large part of 18th-century Rennes. Beyond the perimeter of Old Rennes is a neighborhood of sober, elegant 17th- and 18th-century stone buildings dominated by the Place du Palais, a square of impressive houses set around the Palais de Justice—the Law Courts—once the Houses of Parliament of Brittany.

Just south of the Vilaine, in the center of town, are Rennes's two important museums, the Musée de Bretagne and the Musée des Beaux-Arts.

To the east of Rennes is the Château Les Rochers, where the marquise de Sévigné, the 17th-century author, once wrote her literary letters and entertained hundreds of guests, right. Among the landmarks of old Rennes is the Hôtel de Ville (town hall) with a grand clock in the central tower, inset above right. (Photos: Daniel Gallon)

The master bedroom, with its elegant *faux marbre* door frames, gives onto a small sitting room with two Louis XV armchairs. Beyond is the living room, with a view of a large étagère holding a collection of 18th-century regional faience and porcelain.

In the terra-cotta–tiled second-floor landing, right, an 18th-century oval mirror hangs above an old-fashioned bouquet gathered on the property. A superbly sculpted 18th-century door leads from the landing into a small bed/sitting room. A large 18th-century Beauvais tapestry, woven from a design by Nicolas Poussin, covers one wall of a guest bedroom, below right.

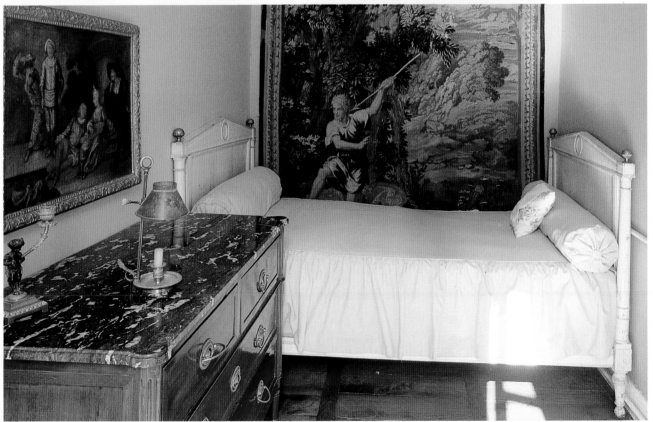

REFURBISHED INSIDE AND OUT

This intimate and meticulously maintained 16th-century château deep in the countryside of Brittany's Ille-et-Vilaine *département*, between Nantes and Angers, is only a shadow of what it once was. In the 18th century a fire destroyed what must have been an imposing château with twin turrets, leaving only one turreted flank intact; only the two lower floors remained in the rest of the structure. Instead of rebuilding the house according to the original plan, the 18th-century owners, deeming the cost of replacing an entire story too great, made the place livable, if not symmetrical, by restoring the lower floors and capping them with a slate roof. The result-

A double-arched stone entry-way, left, leads into a young baron's trim and asymmetrical estate at the eastern limits of Brittany in the Ille-et-Vilaine. The château's ten rooms are divided among the original 16th-century part of the home, to the right above, and the lower 18th-century part, reconstructed after a fire destroyed the top two floors.

ing residence, little changed in succeeding centuries, has an unusual "lazy L" silhouette.

The young baron and baroness who live here today with their two children were given the property by the baron's grandfather in 1970. The estate has been in their family since the late 18th century. Originally built as a noble's château, it became a farm after the Revolution and remained one until the current owner took over the property. "You might say I'm the new king of the castle," says the baron with a laugh. "Since 1970 I've been slowly bringing the place back as a château, restoring the house and the grounds to the way they were in the early 18th century. The next step is to install a new roof on the *porche*

In the living room, left, with antique beams and a sculpted fireplace, a contemporary glass coffee table and a custom-made sofa complement an unmatched grouping of heirloom Louis XV *fauteuils* (armchairs). Afternoon sunlight burnishes a sumptuous array of roses in full bloom, above, freshly cut from the baroness's gardens.

203

[gatehouse], then to replace two massive period doors that disappeared from the *porche* years ago." The château, once virtually empty except for a few pieces of broken farm furniture, has been replenished with inherited antique furnishings and custom-made overstuffed velour sofas.

The baroness, who inherited her green thumb from her father, a *pépiniériste* (professional nurseryman), oversees the plantings and upkeep of the gardens. Her care and talent are evidenced by the lavishly blooming crimson and magenta roses that border the stable and by the flourishing *potager* (vegetable garden) a few yards beyond the lawns at the side of the house. Inside the château, hallways, rooms, and window niches are brightened with sumptuous, freshly cut garden bouquets.

The baroness's massive garden bouquets enliven almost every room in the house, including the entrance foyer with its baroque console, above. A portrait of the baron's grandmother hangs above an ornate desk flanked by two Louis XVI *fauteuils* in the living room, right.

In [...] se[...] vert[...] doo[...] nich[...] than[...] the [...] way[...] ning[...] the [...]

The country kitchen, with its old beams, blue-and-white enamel tiles, and hanging bouquets of dried flowers and herbs, was constructed at the end of the 18th century from components of a chapel on the property. The dining room lies just beyond the kitchen door.

ar
si
rc

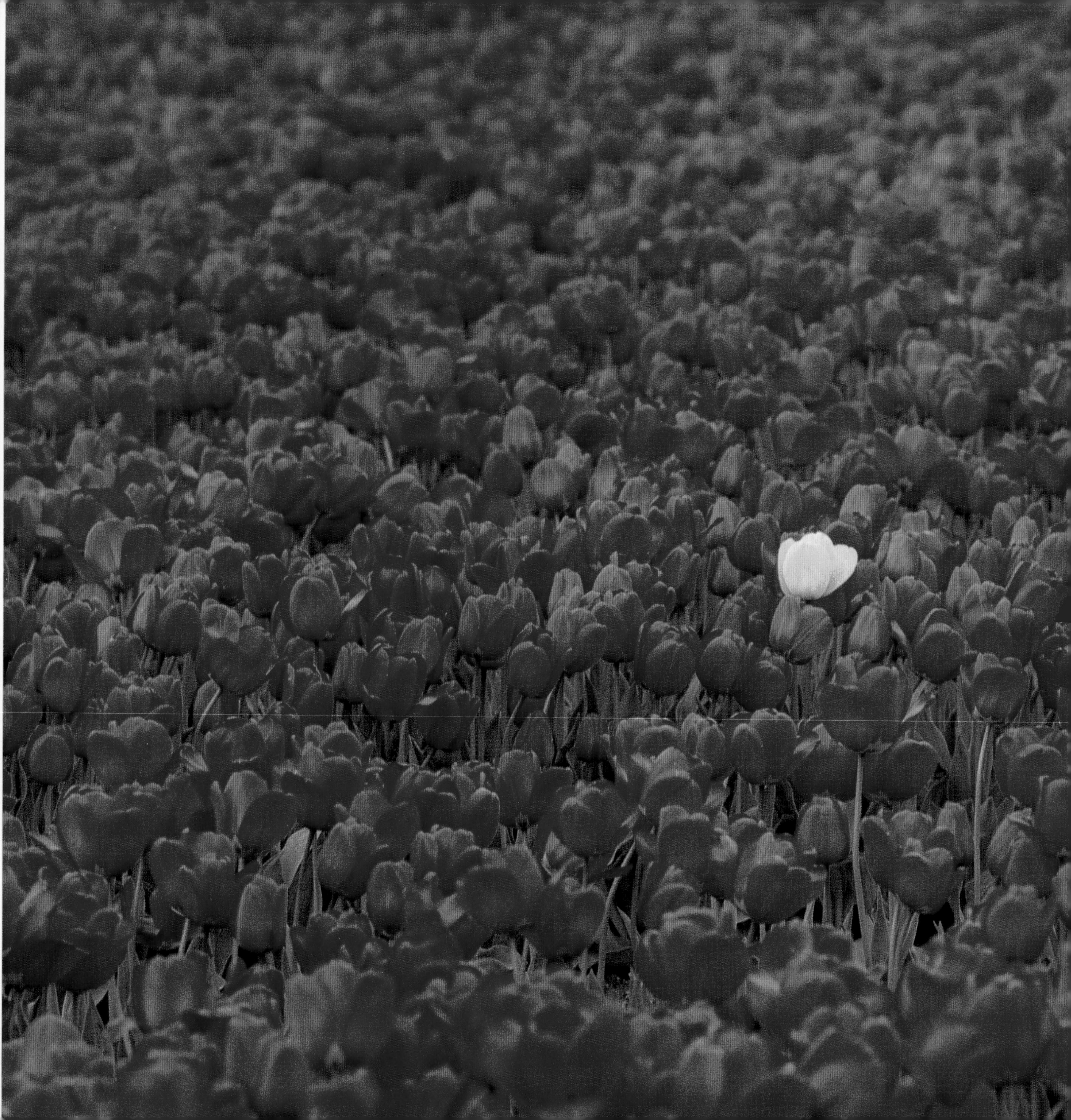

old-fashioned air, Locronan is hardly undiscovered: Roman Polanski filmed *Tess* here a decade ago.

Twenty-one miles due west of Quimper, but well over an hour's drive away, is the glistening white port town of Audierne. Once important for sardine fishing, Audierne now specializes in rock lobster, langoustines, and tuna. Audierne is an unusual port town in that it is set at the foot of steep hills and is surrounded by forests. The tall, whitewashed buildings that ring the port are built in terraced steps up the hilly terrain. Visitors are drawn to Audierne by the wide, white sand beach a mile from town and by the notable harborside restaurant, Le Goyen.

A startling discovery for visitors driving along the sandy dune roads of the Penmarc'h peninsula south of Audierne is a seemingly endless field of tulips, left, planted by entrepreneurs and thriving in the unusual seaside environment. Near the Pointe du Raz, above, a boathouse and small cottage cling to the rocks.

The perfectly preserved town of Locronan, northeast of Quimper, is a 17th-century architectural treasure. The granite houses that surround the cobbled main square were built by wealthy sailmakers in the 1600s, during the town's heyday as prime supplier of sails to the French navy and the Compagnie des Indes. Each home has unique detailing; particular attention has been given to the *lucarnes* (dormer windows), where the stonemason's imagination exulted in arches, scrolls, pediments, dentils, capitals, heraldic emblems, and almost every other element in the artisan's vocabulary.

At La Chaumière, an authentic stone cottage still owned by the Kersaudy family and now open to the public in Audierne, a richly carved suite of 17th- and 18th-century linen chests and *lits clos* lines the north wall of the home's common room, left. Traditionally, the entire extended family slept in this room; the couple with the youngest baby took the *lit clos* nearest to the fireplace. An old advertising poster in the *chaumière*'s foyer, top, urges residents to have themselves photographed in Breton costumes; above, a photograph of the late Madame Kersaudy, taken in the 1920s shortly after she won a local beauty contest.

One of a set of dining chairs, left, in the collection of the Musée Breton in Quimper, is intricately carved with scenes of Breton life and further decorated with spindles and finials—a far fancier form than seen in most Breton homes. The set was designed in 1918 for a local bride.

A detail of a deeply stained and richly patinated oak linen chest, left, dating from the 17th century, is carved—as many pieces of the period were—with angels, hearts, and ornate border detailing.

Carved concentric circles known as the *gâteau* (cake-style) motif adorn a corner of a 19th-century *lit clos*, left. A heavily carved banquette, studded and dated with copper tacks, right, was created near Concarneau as a wedding gift. The spindles of the backrest, turned on a lathe rather than carved, began appearing in Brittany's furniture in the late 19th century.

In the Musée Breton's Paul Fouillen Salon, carved and painted furniture such as this stool and chair, above and right, shows traditional Breton themes as interpreted by this local art deco craftsman whose main body of work was created in the 1930s.

Furniture produced in the 18th and 19th centuries in Audierne and to the west at Pointe du Raz and Cap Sizun —called *capiste* locally—favored floral motifs, right, rather than religious figures.

Geometric and religious motifs, such as the detail of a linen chest, right, are more characteristic of Pont-l'Abbé and Quimper.

227

QUIMPER

Quimper is the old capital of Cornouaille. The town's name derives from the Breton word *kemper* (confluence), since Quimper is lodged at the juncture of the rivers Steir and Odet. The latter, larger river, whose banks are lined with handsome mansions and towering chestnut trees, links Quimper to the sea, just an eleven-mile cruise away.

At Quimper's center is a grand Gothic cathedral, Saint-Corentin, whose soaring twin spires dominate the skyline. Winding off from the Place Saint-Corentin are quaint, narrow streets, such as the rue Kéréon, flanked by tall, half-timbered, medieval houses.

Once a year in the summertime, Quimper hosts one of the largest and liveliest folk festivals in Brittany, La Fête de la Cornouaille. For a full week at the end of July, the town becomes a stage for the program of parades, dances, musical events, and theatrical performances. Regional costumes are everywhere in the streets, as are the busloads of tourists who arrive to witness and to celebrate this happy annual extravaganza.

The twin steeples of Quimper's Saint-Corentin Cathedral, left, set in the town's main square, dominate the skyline of this old capital of Cornouaille, positioned at the confluence of the Steir and Odet rivers. Several old streets that lead into the Place Saint-Corentin, such as the rue Kéréon, right, are still lined with four-hundred-year-old half-timbered houses.

BRETON DESSERTS

Simple, classic meals in Cornouaille often end with one of the dense baked desserts native to the entire province but especially prevalent in this most traditional area. The desserts are dominated by the flavor of fresh salted butter, Brittany's most characteristic dairy product. Butter not only intensifies the flavors of the other main ingredients—sugar, eggs, milk, and flour—but its generous dose of salt helps preserve the desserts for many days.

An assortment of butter-rich Breton desserts is set out for a *goûter*, or snack, at La Chaumière in Audierne, left. Clockwise from the top is a *kouign-amann*, similar to a coffee cake; a *gâteau Breton*, a dense yellow cake; and *gâteaux Bretons*, crumbly cookies. A hand-painted plaque outside a bakery in Locronan, right, announces some of the Breton sweets to be found within.

Nos fabrications maison pur beurre

Le gâteau Breton
nature, aux pruneaux, aux pommes

Le quatre quart
nature et aux pruneaux

Le kouign-Amann

Le far
aux raisins, aux pommes

sola

the

cotta

veys

flow

down t

early 19

niers (se

and dri

pharma

When t

the late

was, as

lutely i

larged i

traditio

the slat

sabelle

tor, abo

isolation o

tion cottag

sea near t

The cotta

a yard left

keeping w

setting an

plicity. In

toration,

to the nor

PORTFOLIO

A Guide to Shopping and Staying in Brittany

Part of the fun of a long, leisurely visit to Brittany is discovering on your own the best foods, crafts, antiques, and sights the region has to offer. A few fortunate visitors have unlimited days for exploration, but most travelers never have time to unearth a province's most intriguing pleasures. Our Portfolio of personal recommendations gives the visitor with limited time a head start on appreciating Brittany's bounty. This guide to the antiques shops, markets, festivals, restaurants, hotels, and sights throughout Brittany is subjective and selective; apart from the extensive listing of regional antiques shops, we mention only a few attractions in each category; we hope you enjoy our favorites and discover others of your own.

Bon voyage en Bretagne!

ANTIQUES

Most of the antiques shops listed here carry a wide variety of merchandise, from fine 18th- and 19th-century furniture to small *objets*, such as faience, lace, and copperware. A few antiques shops also offer reproductions. The *antiquaires* (antiques dealers) are organized by *département*, with regional specialties noted at the top of each section. A star denotes the major *antiquaires* in town.

For serious collectors antiquing in France, the best and most comprehensive guide is the *Guide Emer*. This annual publication lists dealers by region and specialty, including those who specialize in stonework, tile, wrought iron, and lace as well as furniture. The *Guide Emer* is widely available in bookstores throughout France, or can be ordered directly from: *Guide Emer*, 50 rue Quai de l'Hôtel de Ville, 75004 Paris, France. Three other useful antiques publications are the French magazines *ABC Décor*, *Trouvailles*, and *Estampille*, with features on antiques and collectibles, and listings of antiques shows and fairs through-

out France. The magazines are sold in bookstores and at many newspaper stands in Paris and other major French cities.

CÔTES-DU-NORD

In the *département* of the Côtes-du-Nord, *antiquaires* offer heavily sculpted and relatively ornate Breton furniture such as *lits clos*, *buffet-vaisseliers* (buffet with dishrack) armoires, tables, and storage trunks in chestnut or cherry. Many dealers also carry Quimper faience, pewter, and regional copperware, model boats, costumes, and *coiffes*.

BOURSEUL (postal code 22130)
Lelandais Au Bourg.*
Tel. 96 84 03 06.

DINAN (postal code 22100)
Antiquités de Matignon
1 place des Merciers.
Tel. 96 39 01 47.
Greniers du Jerzual (Les)
8 rue de la Poissonnerie.*
Tel. 96 39 74 04.
Guyot 10 rue de l'Hortoge.
Tel. 96 39 29 56.
Lossois-Guido 13 place des Cordeliers.*
Tel. 96 39 11 14.
Pagner-Guido 11 place des Cordeliers.*
Tel. 96 39 54 36.
Pétroff 2 rue de la Larderle.*
Tel. 96 39 51 80.

EVRAN (postal code 22630)
Juette rue de l'Hôpital.
Tel. 96 27 47 49.

GUINGAMP (postal code 22200)
Bourdon 11 rue J.J.-Rousseau.*
Tel. 96 43 91 23.

Danguy 4 rue de l'Yser.
Tel. 96 43 77 31.
Leon 2 rue des Halles.*
Tel. 96 43 71 52.
Maho-Vallée 8 rue du Pot d'Argent.
Tel. 96 44 19 02.

LAMBALLE (postal code 22400)
Temps Jadis (Au) 12 rue du Docteur Calmette.
Tel. 96 34 75 80.

LANNION (postal code 22300)
Cendrillon 4 rue Cie-Roger-Barbé.*
96 37 14 56.
Dépôt Vente du Trégor rue de Plouaret.
Tel. 96 37 18 28.
Le Moal 16 rue Cie-Roger-Barbé.*
Tel. 96 37 66 69.
Louis 5 avenue Ernest-Renan.
Tel. 96 37 42 83.
Mevel rue de Morlaix.*
Tel. 96 46 59 47.

LANVALLAY (postal code 22100)
Source (La) 8 rue du Lion-d'Or.*
Tel. 96 39 44 86.

LANVOLLON (postal code 22290)
Droumaguet 24 place du Marché-au-Blé.
Tel. 96 70 04 29.

LOCQUEMEAU (postal code 22300)
Cornelis le Dou de Bassan

MATIGNON (postal code 22550)
Antiquités le Moulin de la Mer.*
Tel. 96 41 09 19.
Le Calonnec l'Hôpital.
Tel. 96 41 08 35.

PAIMPOL (postal code 22500)
En ce Temps Là 6 rue Saint-Vincent.*
Tel. 96 20 80 35.

PERROS-GUIREC (postal code 22700)
Bonheur des Jours (Au) 40 rue de la Chapelle de la Clarte.*
Tel. 96 23 00 50.
Morgan Tres Traou
Stephan et Crous 66 rue du Mar-Joffre.*
Tel. 96 23 38 63.

PLANCOET (postal code 22130)
Paul 13 rue de Dinard.*
Tel. 96 84 27 57.

PLESLIN (postal code 22490)
Lemée la Bigotière.*
Tel. 96 27 84 76.

PLESTIN-LES-GREVES (postal code 22310)
Levron 28 rue du Pont-Menou.
Tel. 96 35 66 01.

PLOUGUENAST (postal code 22150)
Fichaut Moulin de la Touche.
Tel. 96 28 74 93.
Roinet à Saint-Théo.*
Tel. 96 28 75 68.

PLOURHAN (postal code 22880)
Tharaud-Soudry Ville Allio.
Tel. 96 71 90 60.

PLUMAUGAT (postal code 22250)
Moreau Le Châtel.
Tel. 96 86 68 23.

PLURIEN (postal code 22240)
Allain-Humbert 1 Grand-Rue.*
Tel. 96 72 11 27.

SAINT-BRIEUC (postal code 22000)
André 3 rue Saint-Guéno.*
Tel. 96 61 59 29.
Boscher-Belleissue 2 rue Baratoux.
Tel. 96 33 63 55.
Brocante (La) 17 rue Mal-Foch.
Tel. 96 61 81 95.
Catherine et André 26 rue de Gouédic.
Tel. 96 33 60 13.
Foire au Troc (La) 5 rue Ambroise Croizat
Tel. 96 78 08 72.
Ghin 54 rue de Paris.*
Tel. 96 33 17 48.
Heneaux 25 rue Saint-Guillaume.*
Tel. 96 33 07 90.

SAINT-MELOIR-DES-BOIS (postal code 22980)
Pierre Le Bourg.
Tel. 96 27 09 32.

TREGASTEL (postal code 22730)
Sallou 19 rue du Gal-de-Gaulle.
Tel. 96 23 34 53.

TREGUIER (postal code 22220)
Paternotte 65 rue Renan.*
Tel. 96 92 48 51.

TREMEREUC (postal code 22490)
Delville Sortie du Bourg route Dinard-Dinan.
Tel. 96 27 85 14.

TREVENEUC (postal code 22410)
Maho-Vallée La Ferme de Kerezen.

UZEL (postal code 22460)
Art Déco International place du Martray.
Tel. 96 26 20 02.

VAL-ANDRE (LE) (postal code 22370)
André 40 rue Charner.*
Tel. 96 72 22 90.

ILLE-ET-VILAINE

This rich area for antiques hunters has an abundance of Louis XV–inspired furniture, much of it in cherry: *étagères*, *buffet-deux corps*, *armoires Rennaises*, a variety of *malouines* (Saint-Malo–style) pieces, such as large rectangular armoires with deep molding, pirate chests, and *garde-mangers*. Faience from Quimper, maritime *objets*, and antique weapons are also available.

ARGENTRE-DU-PLESSIS (postal code 35370)

Crosnier 30 rue d'Anjou.
Tel. 99 96 61 88.

BAIN-DE-BRETAGNE (postal code 35470)

Boulle rue de Vitré sur Départementale 777.★
Tel. 99 43 96 03.

Lemoine La Lande Fleurie route de Nantes.★
Tel. 99 43 70 81.

BAIS (postal code 35680)

Galode Les Rochettes.
Tel. 99 76 38 60.

BOURGE-LE-FERRE (postal code 35420)

Battais
Tel. 99 97 02 92.

BRUZ (postal code 35170)

Caradec La Croix-Madame.
Tel. 99 52 64 84.

CANCALE (postal code 35260)

Laick La Houle.
Tel. 99 89 60 76.

Le Bout 5 rue des Trois-Frères.★

CHANTELOUP (postal code 35150)

Templon Le Rocher.★
Tel. 99 44 04 88.

CHANTEPIE (postal code 35135)

Jouanolle 7 rue Nationale.
Tel. 99 50 52 95.

CHAPELLE-DES-FOUGERETZ (LA) (postal code 35520)

Entrepôt des Antiquités (L') La Brosse rue de Saint-Malo.★
Tel. 99 66 41 80.

CHAPELLE-JANSON (LA) (postal code 35133)

Geslin La Pierre.★
Tel. 99 95 20 81.

CHAPELLE–SAINT-AUBERT (LA) (postal code 35140)

Hubeau Brocante du Bois-Gilles R.N. 12.
Tel. 99 98 85 31.

CHATEAUBOURG (postal code 35220)

Perrin ch. du Houpré.
Tel. 99 62 38 47.

CHATEAUGIRON (postal code 35410)

Georget 3 rue de la Madeleine.
Tel. 99 37 81 01.

COMBOURG (postal code 35270)

Erussard allée des Primevères.
Tel. 99 73 03 09.

DINARD (postal code 35800)

Foyer Breton 13 rue Mal-Leclerc.
Tel. 99 46 40 40.

Lecuyer 38 bis rue Mal-Leclerc.
Tel. 99 46 51 80.

Motte 95 bis avenue du Gal-Giraud.
Tel. 99 46 17 35.

Tire la Chevillette 47 rue du Mal-Leclerc.
Tel. 99 46 24 88.

Vergine 15 rue Dumont.

DOL-DE-BRETAGNE (postal code 35120)

Depot-Vente 16 rue P. Flaux.

Laick 27 Grande-Rue.★
Tel. 99 48 04 84.

Mandallaz R.N. 176.
Tel. 99 48 19 80.

FORGES-LA-FORET (postal code 35640)

Drouet à L'Epine.
Tel. 99 47 92 87.

FOUGERES (postal code 35300)

Atelier du Cadre 20 rue Nationale.
Tel. 99 94 06 04.

Battais 2 rue Duguay-Trouin.★
Tel. 99 99 01 66.

Battais 46 boulevard de Rennes.
Tel. 99 99 11 46.
To the trade only.

Bosquain (Le) 9 rue Alexandre III.★
Tel. 99 94 38 04 (AB).

Brocante-Antiquités 53 boulevard de Rennes.
To the trade only.

Gledel (C.) 59 rue Kleber.
Tel. 99 99 00 76.

Gledel 26 rue Canrobert.
Tel. 99 94 08 44.

FOUILLARD (postal code 35340)

Barreau R.N. 12.
Tel. 99 62 04 48.

Beaufils 57 rue Nationale.
Tel. 99 59 06 00.

Quellier Antiquités de la Forêt (La) Jutauderie R.N. 12.
Tel. 99 62 00 34.

GUERCHE-DE-BRETAGNE (LA) (postal code 35130)

Lagrille 18 rue Neuve.
Tel. 99 96 41 41.

GUICHEN (postal code 35580)

Galerie du Boel Jouault.*
Tel. 99 42 21 60.

HEDE (postal code 35630)

Annic 18 place de la Mairie.
Tel. 99 45 41 46.

JANZE (postal code 35150)

Boury Z.A. de la Chauvellère.
Tel. 99 47 26 66.

MARCILLE-ROBERT (postal code 35240)

Barbotin.
Tel. 99 43 67 74.

MELESSE (postal code 35520)

Goriaux 24 rue Saint-Germain.
Tel. 99 66 11 60.

MEZIERE (LA) (postal code 35520)

Prioul (Paul) Les Tallettes rue de Rennes–Saint-Malo.
Tel. 99 66 52 64.
To the trade only.

MINIAC-MORVAN (postal code 35540)

Dauvissat Brocante de la Saboterie.
Tel. 99 58 51 75.

MONT-DOL (postal code 35120)

Papail à la Bassière.
Tel. 99 48 06 49.

NOYAL-SUR-VILAINE (postal code 35530)

Gruel Zone Artisanale 13 rue de la Giraudière.
Tel. 99 00 50 17(B).
To the trade only.

PAIMPONT (postal code 35380)

Brocantik Grande-Rue.
Tel. 99 07 81 53.

PLEINE-FOUGERES (postal code 35610)

Fournier-Battais Mont-Rouault.
Tel. 99 48 60 32.

PLELAN-LE-GRAND (postal code 35380)

Berna Manoir de la Cour du Gué.
Tel. 99 06 97 75.

Mouton 53 rue Nationale.
Tel. 99 06 93 74.

Schamel Les Maisons-Neuves.*
Tel. 99 06 83 05.

PLEURTUIT (postal code 35730)

Delahaye Manoir du Dick.*
Tel. 99 88 42 14.

Le Calonnec la Ville-Aug-Monniers rue de Ploubalay–Saint-Malo.*
Tel. 99 46 25 57.

REDON (postal code 35600)

Bric-à-Brac

RENNES (postal code 35000)

Agora 13 rue Victor-Hugo.*
Tel. 99 38 92 53.

Art Deco 14 rue Victor-Hugo.

Barbay 4 rue de Clisson.
Tel. 99 79 23 65.

Bellion 13 rue du Chapitre.
Tel. 99 79 24 37.

Bric-à-Brac (Au) 44 boulevard Jacques-Cartier.*
Tel. 99 65 44 38.

Chevallier-Clossais 11 rue Victor-Hugo.
Tel. 99 38 86 92.

Couffon de Trevos 15 rue Hoche.
Tel. 99 38 75 95.

Curiosités 27 rue du Guesclin.
Tel. 99 79 18 84.
Also, 2 place Saint-Sauveur.

Durif 3 quai Châteaubriand.*
Tel. 99 79 06 69.

Ferte 7 rue de Juillet.
Tel. 99 31 66 97.

Ferte 14 rue Vasselot.

Grenier d'Anais (Le) 1 rue Salomon-de-Brosse.
Tel. 99 79 56 95.

Lacour Frères 354 rue de Nantes.
Tel. 99 50 24 34.

Le Gallion 228 rue Saint-Malo.
Tel. 99 59 16 00.

Le Golvan 13 rue Saint-Michel.
Tel. 99 79 24 89.

Le Moal 21 rue du Chapitre.*
Tel. 99 30 17 18.

Massicot 9 rue de l'Hortoge.

Perrin 62 rue Châtillon.
Tel. 99 50 54 31.
Also, boulevard Jacques Cartier

Perrin 62 rue de la Chalotais.
Tel. 99 79 08 04.

P'tite Chine (La) 13 rue des Frères-Blin.
Tel. 99 33 73 23.

Salles des Ventes Particuliers (La) 31 boulevard Villebois-Mareuil.
Tel. 99 36 51 51.

Tire la Chevillette 10 rue Derval.*
Tel. 99 38 89 09.

Troc-Antiquité 5 rue François-Elleviou.

Trouillard Antiquités-Expertises 17 rue de la Monnale.
Tel. 99 79 03 68.

Vieux Saint-Melaine (Au) 29 rue Saint-Melaine.
Tel. 99 38 73 32.

SAINT-BRICE-EN-COGLES (postal code 35460)

Laurent 9 rue de Saint-Ouen.
Tel. 99 98 62 17.

SAINT-JEAN-SUR-VILAINE (postal code 35220)

Perrudin Le Pin du Nationale 857.
Tel. 99 62 37 44.

SAINT-LUNAIRE (postal code 35800)

Le Bihan 91 boulevard Gal-de-Gaulle.
Tel. 99 46 35 53.

SAINT-MALO–PARAME–SAINT-SERVAN (postal code 35400)

Barre 8 Grande-Rue.*
Tel. 99 40 89 58(A).

Busnel (Jacques-Henry) 17 rue de Siam.*
Tel. 99 81 60 54.
Also, 4C rue Dauphine.

Busnel (Jacques-Henry) 12 rue de Dinan.*
Tel. 99 40 96 19.

Capisani 8 Grand-Rue.
Tel. 99 40 96 79 (AB).

Couet (Paramé) 37 boulevard Chateaubriand.*
Tel. 99 56 02 48.

Delouche (F.) 2 place de la Cathédrale.
Tel. 99 40 96 60.

Delouche (O.) 3 rue Gouinn-de-Beauchesne.
Tel. 99 40 01 02.

Douet de la Villefromoy 3 rue de la Blatrerie.*
Tel. 99 40 89 19.

Le Morvan 17 rue de Toulouse. Tel. 99 40 86 56. Also, 3 rue des Cordiers.

Manoir de la Perche (Le) (quartier de la Concorde–Saint-Servan) 12 rue P.-Certain.★ Tel: 99 81 97 57.

Moka Antiquités 77 avenue de Moka. Tel. 99 56 29 29.

Nere 17 rue Dauphine.★ Tel. 99 81 18 73.

Noël 11 Grande-Rue. Tel. 99 40 98 82.

Sanneville 1 place de la Cathédrale.★ Tel. 99 40 83 38.

SAINT-MELAINE (postal code 35220)

MAINE-ET-LOIRE

POUANCE (postal code 49420)

Marcel Metzger 84 route de Chateaubriand. Tel. 41 92 62 52.

FINISTÈRE

Oak or chestnut Breton furniture detailed with geometric or religious motifs, spindles, and sometimes copper studs—*lits clos*, farm tables, low armoires, and *bonnetières*—are among the antiques available from dealers in the Finistère. One can also find earthenware and faience from Rennes and Quimper, copperware, paintings from the Pont-Aven school, and nautical collectibles.

BENODET (postal code 29118)

Lasserre 29 avenue de l'Odet. Tel. 98 57 04 09.

Hanten 12 rue des Etangs. Tel. 99 00 30 06.

SAINT-MALOIR-DES-ONDES (postal code 35350)

Vannier Les Portes Rouges. Tel. 99 89 13 45.

SENS-DE-BRETAGNE (postal code 35490)

Fusel Tel. 99 39 51 44.

SIXT SUR AFT (postal code 35550)

Coulon Branfeu. Tel. 99 70 00 92.

THIEL-DE-BRETAGNE (Le) (postal code 35240)

Vilais La Blanchère. Tel. 99 43 55 56.

TRONCHET (LE) (postal code 35540)

Domaine Le Moulin à Vent. Tel. 99 58 91 65.

VITRE (postal code 35500)

Desmontils 36 rue Baudrairie.★ Tel. 99 75 28 34.

Durif 23 rue Notre-Dame.★ Tel. 99 75 22 22.

Trottier 17 & 19 rue Baudrairie.★ Tel. 99 75 04 01.

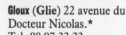

Odet Brocante 23 avenue de l'Odet.★ Tel. 98 55 52 69.

BREST (postal code 29200)

Belle Epoque (La) 35 rue Jean Macé. Tel. 98 46 44 77.

Dare 14 bis rue Yves-Collet.★ Tel. 98 46 23 81.

Droumaguet 29 rue Voltaire. Tel. 98 80 40 90.

Graic 14 rue Louis-Pasteur. Tel. 98 44 86 12.

Grenier de Recouvrance 35 rue Amorique. Tel. 98 45 76 66.

Grenier (Le) 1 ter rue Poullic-al-Lor. Tel. 98 44 54 82.

Grognard (Le) 20 rue du Château. Tel. 98 80 23 15.

Henrio 3 rue Alain Fournier.★ Tel. 98 46 47 81.

Marché des Occasions (Le) 31 rue Yves Collet. Tel. 98 46 12 78.

Mingam 4 rue des 11 Martyrs. Tel. 98 46 44 40.

Patris 19 rue de Glasgow. Tel. 98 80 04 90.

Roger Le Stana à Saint-Anne du Portzic.★ Tel. 98 45 84 34.

Salaun 5 rue Etienne Dolet. Tel. 98 44 57 08.

Samain place de la Tour d'Auvergne. Tel. 98 44 24 34.

CAMARET (postal code 29129)

Sophie Brocante 4 place Saint-Thomas. Tel. 98 27 97 48.

CHATEAULIN (postal code 29150)

Robin 3 place de la Résistance. Tel. 98 86 05 63.

CHATEAUNEUF-DU-FAOU (postal code 29119)

Keraval 37 rue de la Mairie. Tel. 98 81 74 49.

Pasquet 15 rue du Clédig. Tel. 98 81 80 10.

CLOHARS-CARNOET (postal code 29121)

Dulac 4 et 12 rue des Grands Sables.

COMBRIT (postal code 29120)

Courtil (Le) "Kerlec."★ Tel. 98 56 46 64.

Nedelec Botform, C.D. 44.★ Tel. 98 56 36 03.

CONCARNEAU (postal code 29110)

Broc'lyne 19 rue des Ecoles.

Caron 2 rue Vauban. Tel. 96 97 80 96.

Depoid (Glie) 11 rue Vauban.★ Tel. 98 97 30 91 or 98 97 31 36.

Gloux (Glie) 22 avenue du Docteur Nicolas.★ Tel. 98 97 32 23.

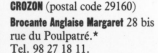

CROZON (postal code 29160)

Brocante Anglaise Margaret 28 bis rue du Poulpatré.★ Tel. 98 27 18 11.

Gueguen 1 rue Louis Pasteur. Tel. 98 27 12 02.

DOUARNENEZ (postal code 29100)

Lebars-Vauzelle 28 rue Duguay-Trouin. Tel. 98 92 18 44.

FAOU (LE) (postal code 29142)

Breiz 15 rue de Landerneau. Tel. 98 81 96 82.

FORET-FOUESNANT (LA) (postal code 29133)

Depôt-Vente route de Fouesnant.

Heure Ancienne (L') 52 Corniche de la Cale. Tel. 98 56 99 46.

FOUESNANT (postal code 29107)

Fornes Ferme de Kerambras route de Beg-Meil. Tel. 98 56 05 24.

Goas place de l'Eglise.*
Tel. 98 56 00 20.

GOUESNOU (postal code 29239)
Patris 50 rue de la Gare.
Tel. 98 07 71 15.

HUELGOAT (postal code 29218)
Bothorel Moulin du Crann.
Tel. 98 99 70 71.

KERLAZ (postal code 29100)
Le Berre plage du Ris.
Tel. 98 92 86 26.

LAMPAUL-GUIMILIAU (postal code 29230)
Hamon 5 place du Villers.
Tel. 98 68 71 65.

LANDERNEAU (postal code 29220)
Abgrall-Chevillier place de la Gare.
Tel. 98 85 03 70.
Duhot 55 quai de Cornouaille.*
Tel. 98 85 01 87.
Gueguen-Kerdraon 1-7 rue La Fayette.
Tel. 98 85 26 58.

LANDIVISIAU (postal code 29230)
Le Gall 4 avenue Foch.
Tel. 98 68 03 00.

LANDREVARZEC (postal code 29112)
Lastennet-Peilliet Au Bourg.
Tel. 98 57 92 17.

LESNEVEN (postal code 29260)
Calvez 27 place du Château.
Tel. 98 21 15 52.

Marec 28 rue du Général de Gaulle.
Tel. 98 83 16 47.

LOCQUIREC (postal code 29241)
Lebrun-Levron 54 rue de l'Eglise.*
Tel. 98 67 42 90.

LOCTUDY (postal code 29125)
Larnicol 62 Grande-Rue.
Tel. 98 87 54 54.

MORLAIX (postal code 29210)
Arguel 23 bis rue de Brest.
Tel. 98 63 20 29.
Casano 31 rue de Paris.*
Tel. 98 88 20 39.
Depôt-Vente 25 rue de Paris.
Tel. 98 63 40 10.
Le Manach 46 rue de Paris.*
Tel. 98 88 02 50.
Treanton 40 rue de Paris.*
Tel. 98 88 07 82.

PLEUVEN (postal code 29170)
Laurent Moulin du Pont route de Bénodet.
Tel. 98 54 63 28.

PLONEOUR (postal code 29120)
Le Guyader route de Plonéour à Quimper.
Tel. 98 87 70 57.

PLONEVEZ-DU-FAOU (postal code 29126)
Nicolas "Kervoël."
Tel. 98 81 82 26.

PLOUIGNEAU (postal code 29234)
Grenier (Le) Prat-al-Lann, ex RN 12.
Tel. 98 88 41 72.
Léon 18 route Nale.
Tel. 98 67 71 46.
Queguiner à Restedern.
Tel. 98 79 80 41.

PONT-AVEN (postal code 29123)
Grenier (Le) route de Rosporden.
Tel. 98 06 03 18.
Lysane-Garel 2 rue des Meunières.
Tel. 98 06 01 58.
Rosot 17 rue du Générale-de-Gaulle.*
Tel. 98 06 01 91.

PONT-L'ABBE (postal code 29120)
Binst 7 rue du Lycée.*
Tel. 98 87 20 99.
Caroline Martre-Nicole Euzen 19 rue Pasteur.*
Tel. 98 87 16 81.

QUIMPER (postal code 29000)

Abbaye-Brocantic, Michel Roullot, 56. quai de l'Odet.*
Tel. 98 55 43 34.
Arts et Civilisations 4 rue Laënnec.*
Tel. 98 95 70 95.
Caron 20 route de Pont-l'Abbé.
Tel. 98 55 68 46.
Cornet à Des (Le) 1 rue Saint-Thérèse.
Tel. 98 53 37 51.

Goubet 13 ter avenue de la Libération.
Tel. 98 90 11 02.
Guiguen-Leberre 7 ter rue des Gentilshommes.
Tel. 98 95 89 67.
Harden 6 rue des Gentilshommes.
Tel. 98 95 11 63.
Laurent 31 bis rue Jean-Jaurès.
Tel. 98 90 09 03.

Le Paul 24 rue des Gentilshommes.*
Tel. 98 95 47 22.
Node 19 rue des Douves.
Tel. 98 95 12 79.
Pesce 39 boulevard de Kerguélen.*
Tel. 98 95 08 10.
Porhiel 22 ch. de Kerlividic.*
Tel. 98 95 14 63.

Richard 17 rue des Boucheries.*
Tel. 98 95 16 05.

Vanhove 14 rue Laënnec.*
Tel. 98 95 88 48.

QUIMPERLE (postal code 29130)

Antique Market Le Poteau Vert route de Pont-Scorff.
Tel. 98 39 10 31.

MORBIHAN

Antiquaires in Morbihan specialize in cherry or chestnut furniture from the Vannes region, although Breton furniture from throughout the province is represented. In addition to traditional *lits clos*, linen chests (*presse-à-lin*), and armoires, one can find hearth benches. *pétrins* kneading tables), clocks, and small wall étagères. Also available are earthenware from Saint-Jean-la-Poterie, faience from Jersey, agricultural implements, copperware, jewelry and buckles in copper or silver, and paintings from the Pont-Aven school.

ARRADON (postal code 56610)

Lobrichon Pen et Men.
Tel. 97 44 02 02.

AURAY (postal code 56400)

Basset 7 place de la République.

Dary-Nozahic à Saint-Goustan 51 rue du Château.*
Tel. 97 56 50 48.

Forges rue Gachotte.
Tel. 24 01 79 97.

Legende des Siècles (La) 5 rue de l'Evêque.*
Tel. 97 56 32 63.

Pinsard 26 avenue Wilson.*
Tel. 97 24 01 40.

Traou Kozh à Saint-Goustan 39 rue du Château.
Tel. 97 56 27 52.

BADEN (postal code 56870)

Prieur Moulin de Pomper.*
Tel. 97 57 11 95.

BAUD (postal code 56150)

Poulain route de Locminé, Kerentrée.*
Tel. 97 51 01 33.

BILLIERS (postal code 56190)

Charbonneau 2 rue de la Pérrière.
Tel. 97 41 56 20.

CARNAC (postal code 56340)

Ferme de Port en Dro à Port en Dro.
Tel. 97 52 15 87.

CLERGUER (postal code 56620)

Mourot-Théry Kéraly.
Tel. 97 32 66 20.

ELVEN (postal code 56250)

Oiseau Rare (L') Kerchoux.*
Tel. 97 53 63 23.

ETEL (postal code 56410)

Bleuzen 49 rue de la Libération.
Tel. 97 55 31 15.

FAOUET (LE) (postal code 56320)

Droual 13 illot de la Congrégation.

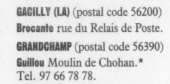

GACILLY (LA) (postal code 56200)

Brocante rue du Relais de Poste.

GRANDCHAMP (postal code 56390)

Guillou Moulin de Chohan.*
Tel. 97 66 78 78.

HENNEBONT (postal code 56700)

Honeywood 24 avenue de la République.
Tel. 97 36 10 35.

JOSSELIN (postal code 56120)

Hecker La Ville Moisan R.N. 24.*
Tel. 97 22 27 45.

Le Corroller 9 rue Saint-Jacques.*
Tel. 97 22 26 97.

KERVIGNAC (postal code 56700)

Le Paih Forme de Lothuen route de Lorient. à Carmac.*
Tel. 97 65 76 89.

LANDEVANT (postal code 56690)

Peron La Brocante au Hameau de Seludierne.
Tel. 97 56 91 94.

LANESTER (postal code 56600)

Mouton Glie Marchande le Rallye.
Tel. 97 76 48 78.

LOCMARIA (postal code 56520)

Mouton.
Tel. 97 65 93 04.

LORIENT (postal code 56100)

Bibicesco Halles Saint-Louis.*

Gall (Le) 43 rue Monistrol.
Tel. 97 37 09 92.

Goullianne 25 rue Larmor.
Tel. 97 64 43 26.

Grenier d'Arthur (Le) 28 rue Gambetta.
Tel. 97 21 70 47.

Il Etait Une Fois 20 rue de Larmor.*
Tel. 97 84 81 07.

Jagorel 88 rue Carnot.
Tel. 97 21 48 44.

Laveyssière 25 rue François-le-Levé.*
Tel. 97 37 71 05.

Lemoussu 15 crs. de la Bove.
Tel. 97 21 55 78.

Livet 10 rue Mal-Foch.
Tel. 97 21 24 74.

Mazeo 9 rue Vauban.
Tel. 97 64 15 76.

Rebière 2 rue Gambetta.*
Tel. 97 21 34 23.

Réminiscence 11 quai des Indes.*
Tel. 97 64 64 99.

Tonnerre 4 rue Marie-Dorval.
Tel. 97 21 82 77.

MERLEVENEZ (postal code 56700)

Chevalley Beg-Er-Lann.*
Tel. 97 65 66 88.

MOREAC (postal code 56500)

Hervo Bourgneuf.
Tel. 97 60 19 96.

PENTHIEVRE (postal code 56510)

Francelet Aux Occasions.
Tel. 97 52 32 73.

PLOEMEUR (postal code 56270)

Bourhis (Gile Saint-Mathurin) route de Lorient.
Tel. 97 82 32 05.

Le Cagnec Loyan route de Guidel.
Tel. 97 82 39 86.

Maillot 5 place de l'Eglise.
Tel. 97 82 37 14.

PLOEREN (postal code 56000)

Vieilleries Le Poulic.
Tel. 97 63 37 73.

PLOUAY (postal code 56240)

Le Stunff 26 rue des Alliés.*
Tel. 97 33 35 81.

PLOUGOUMELEN (postal code 56400)

Bardet Le Kenyah R.N. 165.
Tel. 97 24 11 07.

PLOUHARNEL (postal code 56720)

Le Calvar à Kerfouchelle.*
Tel. 97 52 34 35.

PLUVIGNER (postal code 56330)

Depôt-Vente route de Landevant.

Menut Le Cosquer-Trélécan.*
Tel. 97 24 72 69.

PONTIVY (postal code 56300)

Jego 2 rue Friedland.*
Tel. 97 25 20 21.

Petitcorps 8 rue de Lourmel.*
Tel. 97 25 22 30.

Tugny (de) 10 rue Carnot.*
Tel. 97 27 94 04.

PONT-SCORFF (postal code 56620)

Antiquités-Brocante Kéraly-en-Cléguer.
Tel. 97 32 66 20.

QUIBERON (postal code 56170)

Depôt-Vente de la Presqu'ile
121 rue du Port de Pêche.
Tel. 97 30 44 60.

Frenkiel-Donatien (facing the post office) place de la Duchesse-Anne.*
Tel. 97 50 22 43.

Le Bayon 12 bis rue du Port-Haliguen.
Tel. 97 30 46 65.

ROCHEFORT-EN-TERRE (postal code 56220)

Bon Vieux Temps (Au) Diquero route de Malansac.
Tel. 97 43 32 73.

Brion place du Puit.
Tel. 97 43 31 47.

Danilo Les Grées au Vieux-Bourg.
Tel. 97 43 32 71.

ROCHE-BERNARD (LA) (postal code 56130)

Philippe-Antiquités place de l'Eglise.
Tel. 99 90 60 57.

SAINT-ALLOUESTRE (postal code 56500)

Cattiaux à Toulgouêt.*
Tel. 97 60 37 17

SAINT-NOLFF (postal code 56250)

Menezo-Antiquités à Bellevue, Ancienne route de Rennes.*
Tel. 97 45 43 69.

SARZEAU (postal code 56370)

Chassaniol à Saint-Colombier.
Tel. 97 26 41 50.

Fillion le Vieux Colombier à Saint-Colombier.*
Tel. 97 26 48 46.

Quinio route du Golfe.*

SENE (postal code 56860)

Guillouzic Lande de Cano.
Tel. 97 66 96 18.

Le Layec place de l'Eglise.
Tel. 97 66 90 16.

VANNES (postal code 56000)

Antiquités Madame Damoutte 14 rue Saint-Patern.
Tel. 97 47 17 93.

Antiquités Monsieur Damoutte 87 avenue Edouard Herriot.
Tel. 97 54 33 65.

Bakker (L'Oiseau Rare) 9 rue le Helloc.
Tel. 97 42 49 93.

Cour des Miracles (La) 13 bis rue Porte-Poterne.
Tel. 97 54 16 24.

Goulard 21 rue des Halles.
Tel. 97 54 01 19.

Le Scanff-Sorel 10 rue des Chanoines.
Tel. 97 47 37 93.

Meyer 4 rue de la Bienfaisance.*
Tel. 97 54 31 62(A).

Puces Saint-Patern (Les) 5 rue du Four.
Tel. 97 47 31 91.

Sergent 10 rue Abel-Leroy.
Tel. 97 54 20 47.

ANTIQUES FAIRS AND MARKETS

For precise dates, contact the Bureau de Tourisme in each town, or the French National Tourist Office, 630 Fifth Avenue, New York, New York 10019.

Brest: Foire à la Brocante (Antiques/Second-Hand Goods Fair), first weekend in March.

Hôtel de Ventes (auction house), 26 rue du Château, sales Tuesdays at 2 P.M. and 9 P.M.

Marché aux Puces (flea market), Halles de Récouvrance, Saturdays 9 A.M. to 7 P.M.

Quimper: Salle de Ventes (auction house), 7 boulevard de Kerguélen, sales Wednesdays at 2 P.M.

Rennes: Foire à la Ferraille, à la Brocante et aux Jambons (Ironwork, Second-Hand Goods, and Ham Fair), Parc des Expositions, in June.

Marché aux Puces (flea market), end of January.

Marché aux Puces (flea market), rue Saint-Georges, first and third Saturdays of each month.

Saint-Brieuc: Hôtel de Ventes (auction house), 10-12 rue de Gouét, sales Thursdays at 2 P.M.

Saint-Malo: Marché à la Brocante (Antiques/Second-Hand Goods Market), within the city walls, first Friday of each month.

Vannes: Marché aux Puces (flea market), around Saint-Patern church, first Saturday of each month, 8 A.M. to 4 P.M.

Salle de Vente (auction house), 9 rue Saint-Guenhaël, sales every Saturday at 2 P.M.

FESTIVALS, FAIRS, AND RELIGIOUS EVENTS

Dates for these annual events often change from year to year. For precise dates, contact the Bureau de Tourisme in each town, or the French National Tourist Office, 630 Fifth Avenue, New York, New York 10019.

MAY
Tréguier: Pardon of St. Yves, third Sunday of the month.

Combourg: Fêtes des Fleurs (Flower Festival).

Mont-Saint-Michel: Fêtes de Printemps (Springtime Festival).

JUNE
Camaret-sur-Mer: Benediction de la Mer.

Douarnenez: Benediction de la Mer.

Fougères: Festival des Lutins (Festival of the Elves).

Quimperlé: Grande Fête Folklorique (Grand Folkloric Festival), Whitsunday.

Rennes: Fêtes de la St. Jean (Saint John's Festival).

Saint-Brieuc: Exposition Canine Internationale (International Dog Show), Parc des Expositions.

JULY
Locronan: La Troménie St. Ronan (High mass and procession), second Sunday of the month.

Pont-l'Abbé: Fêtes des Brodeuses (Embroiderers' Festival), second Sunday of the month.

Fouesnant: Fête des Pommiers (Fruit Tree Festival), third Sunday of the month.

Saint-Cast: Fête Folklorique (Folkloric Festival), July 14.

Quimper: Grandes Fêtes de la Cornouaille (Grand Festival of Cornouaille), fourth Sunday of the month and preceding week.

Sainte-Anne-d'Auray: Grand Pardon, July 26.

Combourg: Fête de Nuit au Château (Nighttime Festival at the Château).

Concarneau: Fête de la Mer (Festival of the Sea).

Douarnenez: Fêtes des Mouettes (Seagull Festival).

Ile de Molène: Bénédiction de la Mer et Pardon (Benediction of the Sea and Pardon).

Tréguier: Grandes Fêtes Folklorique (Grand Folkloric Festival).

AUGUST
Pont-Aven: Fête des Ajoncs d'Or (Festival of the Golden Gorse), first Sunday of the month through the following week.

Audierne: Fête des Bruyères (Heather Festival), second Sunday of the month.

Lorient: Fête Interceltique (Inter-Celtic Festival), Early August, one week.

Vannes: Fête de l'Arvor (Festival of the Arvor), August 15.

Le Guilvinec: Fête de la Mer (Festival of the Sea), August 15.

Concarneau: Fête des Filets Bleues (Festival of the Blue Nets), second to last weekend of the month.

Paimpol: Fête de la Paimpolaise (Paimpolaise Festival).

Penmarc'h: Fête des Cormorans (Festival of the Cormorants).

Port-Manech: Fête de l'Aven (Festival of the Aven).

Saint-Briac: Fête des Mouettes (Seagull Festival).

Sainte-Anne-la-Palud: Grand Pardon, last weekend of the month.

SEPTEMBER
Le Folgoët: Grand Pardon, first Sunday of the month.

Josselin: Pardon de Notre Dame du Roncier (Pardon of Our Lady of the Bramblebush), September 9.

Pont-l'Abbé: Fête de la Treminou (Treminou Festival), fourth Sunday of the month.

Mont Saint-Michel: Fête de l'Archange (Festival of the Archangel).

Ouessant: Pèlerinage a Notre Dame de Bon Voyage (Pilgrimage to Our Lady of Safe Travel).

WEEKLY MARKETS

Fresh local produce is colorfully displayed and sold at small stands in these markets.

Belle-Ile: Tuesday and Friday.

Brest: daily, except Monday.

Carnac: Wednesday and Sunday.

Concarneau: Monday and Friday.

Dinan: Thursday.

Dinard: Tuesday, Thursday, and Saturday.

Douarnenez: Monday and Friday.

Le Guilvinec: Tuesday.

Guingamp: Tuesday, Friday, and Saturday.

Landerneau: Tuesday, Friday, and Saturday.

Locmariaquer: Tuesday and Saturday.

Lorient: Wednesday and Saturday.

Morlaix: Saturday morning.

Ploërmel: Monday and Friday.

Pont-l'Abbé: Tuesday through Saturday.

Pont-Aven: Tuesday.

Quimper: Wednesday and Saturday.

Rennes: Saturday.

Riec-sur-Belon: Wednesday.

Saint-Malo: daily, except Sunday.

Trinité-sur-Mer: Tuesday and Friday.

Vannes: Wednesday and Saturday.

WHAT TO SEE AND DO

In Brittany, as in any of France's wonderfuly rich and diverse provinces, we recommend that you travel, time permitting, on the smallest roads possible. These are designated with the letter *D* on the fine-grain maps of the region. The D63, for instance, leads from Locronan to the village of Sainte-Anne-la-Palud. For visiting the province in depth, the green Michelin *Tourist Guide to Brittany* is indispensable as is Michelin's regional map #230, "Bretagne."

Among the sights and activities we urge you not to miss are:

Mont Saint-Michel: the town, the Abbey, and the hotel-restaurant La Mère Poulard.

Cap Fréhel: one of the most dramatic coastal sites in Brittany, with soaring cliffs in shades of charcoal, russet, and ebony rising above the Channel surf.

The islands of Ouessant and Sein: two islands out of time, where life has made few concessions to the 20th century.

Pointe de Raz and the Pointe du Van: two spectacular and sometimes treacherous viewpoints where the sea, in an unforgettable display of power and fury, explodes against the cliffs.

The traditional Breton towns with distinct character and architectural integrity: Locronan, Dinan, Saint-Malo, Guingamp, Quimper, Combourg, La Roche-Bernard, Rochefort-en-Terre.

Beaches: Hundreds of beaches are carved into the Breton coast, from Dinard's cliffside Saint-Enogat beach to La Baule's vast

tract of fine white sand extending almost three miles. Among the nicest spots we discovered are the duneside and oceanside beaches of Beg-Meil, a small resort in south Finistère sheltered by towering pines; and the broad, dune-banked beaches that curve around the Pointe de Penmarc'h.

The Calvaires, Brittany's memorable religious monuments that illustrate with scores—even hundreds—of figures the Passion of Christ: in Plougonven, Plougastel-Daoulas, Pleyben, Guimiliau, and Saint-Thégonnec.

Pont-Aven's hilltop Trémalo Chapel, with its beguiling ensemble of 16th-century polychrome grotesques carved along the beams.

Boat trips: No one can fully experience Brittany without at least one voyage on water. Choose from many short boat rides throughout the province, from the occasionally wild and woolly journey from Brest to Ouessant to the calm and lovely ride up the Odet River from the Atlantic to Quimper. Others include the ride from Dinard to Dinan on the Rance; the three-hour Channel trip to Cap Fréhel from Dinard; and the cruise around the Morbihan islands from Vannes.

Carnac: with its haunting legions of more than 3,000 megalithic monuments.

The impressive, powerfully constructed châteaux de Josselin, Fougères, Vitré, and Combourg in the Ille-et-Vilaine and the Château de Rosanbo in the Côtes-du-Nord.

A handful of intriguing museums, some extensive, some petite, that specialize in exhibits on Breton life, culture and history: the Musée Bigouden in Pont-l'Abbé; the Musée Breton in Quimper; the Musée de la Bretagne in Rennes; the Musée Jacobins in Morlaix; the ecomusée at Niou-Huella on the island of Ouessant; the Musée de la Pêche, a fascinating fishing museum in Concarneau; and the Musée de Saint-Malo in Saint-Malo.

VISITING BRITTANY

WHERE TO STAY

With the exception of La Reine Hortense in Dinard, all of the following hotels have fine restaurants that serve both lunch and dinner, and all welcome outside guests. As with most restaurants in France, reservations are always recommended.

La Belle Etoile. 29110 Le Cabellou-Plage, Concarneau. Tel. 98 97 05 73. A delightful white harborside hotel in south

Finistère set in a shady glen with a view across the water to Concarneau and beaches just steps away.

Hotel de Bretagne. 56230 Questembert. Tel. 97 26 11 12. A tranquil hotel in inland Morbihan with plush rooms decorated with English antiques and a superb oak-panelled restaurant displaying collections of antique glassware and faience.

Château de Locguénolé. 56700 Hennebont. Tel. 97 76 29 04. A handsome château-hotel on a grand property in Morbihan five miles from the coast. Run by the formidable Madame de la Sablière, with well-furnished rooms accented with beamed ceilings, some with fireplaces.

Hotel Coätguélan. 22290 Pléhédel, Lanvollon. Tel. 96 22 31 24. A small, handsomely landscaped château-hotel in the Côtes-du-Nord furnished with regional antiques, with riding, fishing, and golf on the property.

Hôtel de l'Europe. 29210 Morlaix. Tel. 98 62 11 99. In the heart of Morlaix in the Côtes-du-Nord, an old but modernized hotel with plain, comfortable rooms within walking distance of the market square and the town's ancient streets.

Hôtel de la Plage. 29129 Sainte-Anne-la-Palud, Plomodiern. Tel. 98 92 50 12. A pleasant hotel, set in the sand dunes of a tiny town in south Finistère, with small, attractive rooms, many with outstanding views of the sea.

La Mère Poulard, 50116 Mont Saint-Michel. Tel. 33 60 14 01. Somewhat dated, but full of charm, the rooms of the Hôtel La Mère Poulard (there are also three larger, more contemporary suites) are perfect for overnighting on this wonder of the world.

Le Reine Hortense. 35800 Dinard. Tel. 99 46 54 31. A sumptuous, turn-of-the-century villa with Belle Epoque furnishings and decor (including the silver bathtub of Queen Hortense, mother of Napoleon III, in one

room), set directly overlooking the wide sandy Grande Plage, with views across the bay to Saint-Malo.

WHERE TO EAT

Audierne
Restaurant du Goyen, place Jean-Simon. Tel. 98 70 08 88.

Cancale
Restaurant de Bricourt, 1 rue du-Guesclin. Tel. 99 89 64 76.

Concarneau
La Coquille, 1 rue du Moros. Tel. 98 97 08 52.

Le Galion, Ville Close, 15 rue-Saint-Guénolé. Tel. 98 97 30 16.

Dinan
La Caravelle, 14 place Duclos. Tel. 96 39 00 11.

Guingamp
Le Relais du Roy, 42 place du Centre. Tel. 96 43 76 62.

Hennebont
Château de Locguénolé, route de Port-Louis. Tel. 97 76 29 04.

Morlaix
Restaurant de l'Europe, 1 rue d'Aiguillon. Tel. 98 62 11 99.

Pont-Aven
Moulin de Rosmadec, town center. Tel. 98 06 00 22.

La Taupinière, route de Concarneau. Tel. 98 06 03 12.

Questembert
Restaurant Georges Paineau, 13 rue Saint-Michel. Tel. 97 26 11 12.

Rennes
Le Corsaire, 52 rue d'Antrain. Tel. 99 36 33 69.

Le Galopin Gourmet, 21 avenue Jean-Janvier. Tel. 99 30 09 51.

Le Palais, 7 place du Parlement. Tel. 99 79 45 01.

Riec-sur-Belon
Chez Jacky, port du Belon. Tel. 98 06 90 32.

Melanie, place de l'Eglise. Tel. 98 06 91 05.

Sainte Anne-la-Palud
Restaurant de la Plage. Tel. 98 92 50 12.

Saint-Malo
La Duchesse Anne, Ville Close, 5 place Guy-La Chambre. Tel. 99 40 85 33.

Ile de Sein
Auberge des Sénans. Tel. 98 70 90 01.

INDEX